Have a Java

HAVE A JAVA

The ultimate recipe guide for specialty coffees and your favorite Café food

Maggie Siewers

iUniverse, Inc.
New York Lincoln Shanghai

Have a Java

The ultimate recipe guide for specialty coffees and your favorite Café food

Copyright © 2007 by Maggie Siewers

All rights reserved. No part of this book may be used or reproduced by any means, graphic, electronic, or mechanical, including photocopying, recording, taping or by any information storage retrieval system without the written permission of the publisher except in the case of brief quotations embodied in critical articles and reviews.

iUniverse books may be ordered through booksellers or by contacting:

iUniverse
2021 Pine Lake Road, Suite 100
Lincoln, NE 68512
www.iuniverse.com
1-800-Authors (1-800-288-4677)

The views expressed in this work are solely those of the author and do not necessarily reflect the views of the publisher, and the publisher hereby disclaims any responsibility for them.

ISBN: 978-0-595-43296-7 (pbk)
ISBN: 978-0-595-87636-5 (ebk)

Printed in the United States of America

I dedicate this book to Peter for his loving support and encouragement. I will be eternally grateful for his impressive, natural born, taste testing abilities. This book would not have been possible without him.

Contents

Introduction xiii

Coffee Info and Techniques 1
Filter coffee • Espresso • Specialty coffees • Textured milk

Milk Texturing 4
Texturing milk • Steaming milk • Frothing milk • Texturing milk without a machine

Specialty Coffees and Beverages 7
Espressos: Espresso • Dopio • Lungo • Ristretto • Americano • Macchiato • Breve • Con panna • Corretto • Romano • Spicy Viennese • Red eye
Cappuccino Coffees: Cappuccino • Mochaccino • Soyaccino • Iced cappuccino • Frappe
Latte Coffees: Caffe latte • Mocha latte • Flavored latte • Viennese • Caramel Viennese • Caffe mocha • Chai latte • 3 layer latte • 5 Layer latte • Gingerbread latte • Eggnog latte • Mango latte • Steamer

Hot Chocolates 14
Bittersweet hot chocolate • White hot chocolate

Coffee Cocktails 16
Espresso martini • Martini-ccino • Café Napoleon • Café Yukatan • Latte royale • Creamy dreamy martini • Affogato • Con leche shake • Coffee cream whiskey

- vii -

Biscottis 19

    Orange Cranberry • Triple Chocolate • Almond •

    Orange Chocolate • Chocolate Pistachio

Scones 26

    Blueberry scones • Apple date scones • Orange chocolate chip scones • Oatmeal scones • Raisin scones • Maple syrup butter

Muffins 33

    Lemon poppyseed muffins • Rhubarb muffins • Triple chocolate muffins • Tropical carrot muffins • Cranberry orange muffins • Oatmeal date muffins • Blueberry muffins

Sweet Loaf Breads 42

    Banana bread • Carrot bread • Lemon nut bread •

    Financier • Irish Cream pound cake • Cinnamon buns

Cookies 50

    Peanut butter and oatmeal cookies • White chocolate, coconut and macadamia cookies • Chocolate ginger cookies •

    Classic chocolate chip cookies • Oatmeal raisin cookies • Sugar cookies • Chocolate macaroons

Squares and Bars 59

    Gooey fudgey peanut butter brownies • Blondies •

    Chocolate peanut butter squares • Date squares • Butter bars • Oat cakes • Triple chocolate brownies •

    Chocolate buttercream • White chocolate buttercream

Cake Squares 70

    Chocolate banana cake • Orange walnut streusel cake • Lemon blueberry cake • Praline cake • Chocolate CocaCola cake

Pies 78

    Pecan bourbon pie • Double key lime pie • Mile high apple pie • Rhubarb almond tart • Fruit and cream tart • Coconut cream pie • Raisin butter tarts • Perfect pastry dough

Desserts 87

Rice pudding • Bread pudding with bourbon sauce • Crème brulée • No bake cheesecake cups • Mojito granita • Fruit and yogurt parfait

Cakes 99

Tiramisu • Cinnamon streusel coffe cake • Whiskey tipsy fudge cake • Chocolate amaretto cake • Mango Tango carrot cake • Skyscraper chocolate caramel cake • Coco Bango coconut cake • Creamy cheesecake

Breakfast 110

Bagel with ricotta • Moka butter • Bacon and egg baguette • Ham and brie croissant • Nutella banana crêpes • Apricot brandy crêpes • Morning glory ham and eggs

Quiche 117

Bacon and leek quiche • Killer crab quiche • Spinach, mushroom and bacon quiche • Three cheese asparagus quiche • Hot and spicy quiche dough • Tex-Mex quiche • Italian tomato and heart of palm quiche • Olive oil quiche dough

Soups 126

Cream of carrot soup • Lentil and tomato soup • Bangkok soup • Escargot and mushroom soup • Arizona corn and red pepper soup • Cream of heart of palm soup • Onion Soup "au gratin"

Soup Garnishes 134

Cheddar toast • Lace cheese crisps • Eggplant chips • Herbed barley • Cheese straws

Salads 139

Orange fennel salad • Chicken Thai salad • Bowtie pasta salad with pesto, olives and sun dried tomatoes • Greek salad • Cool cucumber mint salad • Spinach couscous salad • Roasted curried harvest vegetable salad

Sandwiches 149

Caramelized onion baguette • Roast beef and blue cheese rolls • Pressed vegetable rolls • Arancini • Bruschetta and brie baguette • Italian panini • Eggplant, hummus and feta ciabatta •

Smoked salmon pumpernickel club

Index 161

Acknowledgements

I have to thank and recognize the following people: Joel Lebeau, Katia Lane, Madison Hantz, Bailey Laskie and all the good people at the "ShmoozeKatz."

Introduction from the author

I wish there had been a book like this when I was opening my first Café-Bistro. I was under the assumption that there was some universal standard by which I could base my recipes for specialty coffees. Wrong! I quickly learned that each Coffee House establishes its own standard. A mochaccino, for example, might be significantly different in taste and volume from one restaurant to another.

Not wishing to disappoint my customers or risk seeing them stand before me with a cup in their hand saying "This isn't what I ordered!" or "When I ask for a Chococcino at "The Corner Bistro" it's three times as big as this and tastes like a milkshake!", I decided, by comparative research, to come up with a list of recipes that can act as an acceptable guideline for European–style coffees. This worked out very successfully for us at the Café.

The menu, however, had to be unique to us and knock down delicious. Everything from our muffins, to our sandwiches, to our cakes had to be so good that people would want to come back time and time again and always leave happy and satisfied.

The results are in this book and I offer them to everyone who has come into the Café and said "This is the best (pie) (panini) (soup) I've ever tasted! Is there any way I could have this recipe?" I offer them to anyone who has gone out and bought a fancy espresso machine but isn't having any success in frothing the milk or making the same specialty coffees as their favorite coffee shop. I also offer them to you, dear reader, so now you can transform your home into your favorite Coffee House whenever you want to.

So, whip up some scones and biscottis, light up the fireplace and put on some jazzy-blues music. Then invite a few of your friends over for cappuccinos and lattes. That stimulating aroma of coffee and pastries fresh from the oven, the happy chatter of friends and family–that is the essence of "Have a Java".

Maggie Siewers

Coffee Info and Techniques

FILTER COFFEE

There are really only two things you need to remember to make a consistently good pot of coffee. First, you need to start with good quality coffee beans. Cheap, bitter coffee beans will produce a bitter pot of coffee. Logical? Secondly, you need to measure! A good rule to follow is 1 tablespoon of finely ground coffee to 1 cup of water. Following these two rules faithfully will give you a good pot of coffee every time. Simple!

ESPRESSO

The word "espresso" comes from the Italian word "express" because it is made and served immediately. If you are interested in the technical definition of an espresso, here it is:

Espresso is produced when 1½ oz of water, at 195º F, is forced under 9 atmostpheric pressure through ¼ oz of finely ground coffee in approximately 25 seconds.

The 'Crema' is the cream that is formed on the top of the coffee when the released coffee oils come into contact with the oxygen in the atmosphere.

Espresso is usually served in a "demitasse" which holds 3 oz of liquid.

COFFEE BEANS

The choice of coffee beans is a matter of taste and preference with most Coffee Houses opting for a coffee blend of 80 percent arabica and 20 percent robusta. It's important to grind the beans just before brewing the coffee for optimal freshness. Most people prefer a fine or extra fine grind so if you are using a home grinder, grind no more than one quarter cup of beans at a time for anywhere between 20–30 seconds. For storage of coffee beans, purchase only the amount you will be requiring for one week and keep the beans in an airtight container. Do not store them in the refrigerator as it is not the appropriate temperature for storing coffee beans and they will absorb odor. Whole beans can be stored in the freezer or at room temperature.

ESPRESSO MACHINES

Most households use the traditional *stovetop espresso or moka pot* . Since the method used produces only half of the ideal 9 bars of pressure, the resulting espresso may lack the crowning crema but it will still give you a rich, flavorful cup of espresso and permit you to make delicious specialized coffees. Another popular home brewer is the *Neapolitan flip-drip* which will give you much the same results as the moka pot except for a slightly stronger coffee. The sophisticated *Pump espresso machines* are a high tech, commercial type version that are becoming increasingly popular for home use despite the hefty price tag.

TAMPING

Tamping is the use of a tamper to compact the ground coffee in the portafilter. The tamper must be applied straight, not on an angle, for the grinds to be evenly packed. The way you can tell if you have applied the right amount of pressure is to examine the wet grounds after you have knocked them out of the portafilter. They should hold together to form a puck and not fall apart into a mushy mess.

SPECIALTY COFFEES

Most specialty coffees use either a single or double dose of espresso as their base to which you can add milk, (steamed, frothed or cold) cream, whipped cream, chocolate flavored syrup, alcohol, spices—to name but a few.

Coffee Info and Techniques   3

Milk Texturing

TEXTURED MILK

Steaming or frothing milk is also referred to as "texturing" the milk. This is the essential part in preparing such specialty coffees as "cappuccinos" or "caffe lattes." This is a technique that is easy and pleasurable to learn and is practiced by barista's–espresso coffee professionals–all over the world. Mastering this technique takes little more than practice and will reward you and yours with a lifetime of wonderful coffee moments.

TEXTURING THE MILK

First, begin with very cold milk and a very cold frothing pitcher. You can keep your stainless steel frothing pitcher in the refrigerator so that it is always ready to be used.

The type of milk you choose depends on your taste. Of course, the more fat there is in your milk, the more flavor there will be. Skim milk produces the fastest, lightest foam. Most restaurants use 2% milk as a happy balance between taste and a beautiful, frothy foam.

Start with fresh milk for every cup, don't reuse leftovers.

STEAMING MILK

Fill the frothing pitcher two thirds full. Clip a thermometer into the pitcher. Insert the steam wand near the bottom of the pitcher. Turn on the steam wand fully and turn it off when the milk has reaches 170º F. Tap the pitcher gently on the countertop to remove any large bubbles which may have formed.

FROTHING MILK

Fill the frothing pitcher one third full. Clip a thermometer into the pitcher. Insert the steam wand so the tip is just beneath the surface of the milk. Turn on the steam wand fully. As the milk rises, lower the pitcher so the wand always remains near the surface of the milk. When the thermometer registers 140º F, plunge the wand down near the bottom of the pitcher. (this "rolling" process gives the foam more texture and thickness) Turn off the steamer when the milk reaches 170º F.

Always be sure to wipe the steam nozzle thoroughly with a clean, damp cloth to prevent bacteria buildup. Next, turn on the steam valve to flush out any milk in the wand.

TEXTURING MILK WITHOUT A MACHINE

If your espresso machine doesn't come with a steam wand, don't worry! You don't really need one. If you own a wire whisk, you're good to go!

Pour cold milk into a saucepan (no more than half way). Place the pan over medium heat. Begin to whisk, slowly at first, then increasing in speed as the milk temperature rises but never allowing the milk to boil.

Remove the pan from the heat source and continue whisking until the consistency of the foam is appropriate to your needs. Let the milk rest for about thirty seconds. This permits the steamed milk and the foamed milk to separate from each other.

This foolproof method, using only a whisk and milk in a saucepan, produces excellent results every time.

* * * *

An alternative method is to use a plunger pot–such as a "Bodum". Simply heat one cup of milk, either on the stovetop or in the microwave, until hot but not boiling. Transfer the milk to the plunger pot and pump for 1–2 minutes or until the milk is thickened and frothy.

Specialty Coffees and Beverages

ESPRESSO

Espresso:

A single shot–approximately 1 to 1½ oz of espresso.

Espresso Doppio (Double Espresso):

A double shot–approximately 3 oz of espresso served in a cappuccino cup.

Espresso Lungo (or Allonge):

A pulled or weakened espresso because it is made with 1-2 oz more water than a regular espresso.

Espresso Ristretto (Short):

A single shot–with less than the usual amount of hot water. (less than 10 oz)

Espresso Americano:

A single shot–to which enough hot water has been added (around 6 oz) to resemble a regular, American-style, cup of coffee.

Espresso Machiatto:

A single shot–topped with a dollop of frothed milk.

Espresso Breve:

A single shot–to which steamed half and half has been added.

Espresso Con Panna:

A single shot–topped with a dollop of whipped cream.

Espresso Corretto:

A single shot–to which 1 oz of liqueur has been added such as Grappa, Sambuca, Brandy, Cognac, etc.

Espresso Romano:

A single shot–served with a twist of lemon or topped with fresh lemon peel.

Spiced Viennese Espresso:

A double shot of espresso mixed with ½ tsp cinnamon, ½ tsp ground cloves, ½ tsp nutmeg.

Red Eye:

A cup of brewed coffee to which a shot of espresso has been added.

Specialty Coffees and Beverages 9

CAPPUCCINO

Cappuccino:

One third espresso, one third steamed milk, one third frothed milk. May be garnished with a sprinkle of cocoa or cinnamon.

Mochaccino:

One third espresso, one third steamed chocolate milk, one third frothed chocolate milk. Garnish with a sprinkle of cocoa.

Soyaccino:

One third espresso, one third steamed soy milk, one third frothed soy milk.

Iced Cappuccino:

A double shot of espresso poured into a glass of ice to which 6 oz's of milk is added. Sweeten to taste.

Cappuccino Frappé:

Basically an iced cappuccino to which sugar or vanilla syrup has been added and then whipped up in a blender.

These two cold cappuccinos are often confused for one another. The iced cappuccino is the classic that Europeans are used to, whereas a North American who orders an iced cappuccino is usually expecting a frappé. Whipped cream and chocolate shavings can top a frappé turning it into an ice cream parlor treat.

Specialty Coffees and Beverages 11

CAFFE LATTE
Caffe Latte:

A double shot of espresso to which steamed milk is added to fill a 9 oz latte bowl.

Mocha Latte:

A double shot of espresso to which steamed chocolate milk is added to fill a 9 oz latte bowl. Add a sprinkle of cocoa.

Flavored Latte:

A caffe latte flavored with about 4 squirts of Italian syrup such as almond, hazelnut, vanilla, etc.

Viennese:

A caffe latte topped with whipped cream and chocolate syrup.

Caramel Viennese:

A caffe latte topped with whipped cream and caramel syrup.

Caffé Mocha:

A single shot of espresso mixed with a spoonful of chocolate syrup and steamed milk. This mixture is poured into a tall glass and topped with whipped cream and shaved chocolate.

Chai Latte:

A popular Zen tea beverage.

To 1 cup strong black tea, add ½ cup milk which has been steamed with 1 tablespoon cinnamon syrup, 1 tablespoon almond syrup, 1½ teaspoons vanilla syrup. Sweeten with 1 teaspoon honey and sprinkle with cinnamon.

3 Layer Latte:

Very elegant!

Fill a glass $2/3$ full with frothed milk. Slowly drizzle a single shot of espresso down the inside rim of the glass. Wait a few moments and the graduation of coffee and milk will make itself. Top with more frothed milk.

5 Layer Latte:

Spectacular and delicious!

In a tall glass, layer 1 oz chocolate syrup, 3 oz steamed milk, a single shot of espresso drizzled slowly down the inside rim of the glass, 3 oz frothed milk, some whipped cream and a sprinkle of cocoa.

The only thing to remember about making layered drinks is to add the espresso slowly. You can also use a spoon to send the espresso against the interior side of the glass. Be sure to always use a clear, heat resistant, beverage glass because the layered effect must be visible.

Gingerbread Latte:

Mix a double shot of espresso with 4 squirts of ginger syrup in a latte bowl. Add steamed milk and sprinkle with cinnamon or crushed gingerbread cookies.

Eggnog Latte:

A holiday delight!

To a double shot of espresso in a latte bowl, add steamed eggnog. (or milk which has been steamed with 1½ oz eggnog syrup) Top with whipped cream and a sprinkle of nutmeg.

Mango Latte:

A caffeine free smoothie.

In a blender, put 1 cubed mango, a few ice cubes, 1 teaspoon sugar and 8oz buttermilk. Blend for 30 seconds.

Steamer:

This drink lets kids enjoy coffee time with their parents.

Steamed milk to which any flavored liquor may be added. May also be topped with whipped cream.

Hot Chocolates

Bittersweet Hot Chocolate:

In a medium saucepan, combine;
    5 oz semisweet chocolate, coarsely chopped
    a pinch of salt
    $1/3$ cup boiling water
Stir until the chocolate melts. Add:
    $2/3$ cup boiling water

Stir over medium heat until it starts to simmer at the edges. Whisk in:
    1 cup whole milk
Whisk constantly until it is steaming hot but not boiling. Let guests add their own sugar, to taste, and pass around a bowl of lightly sweetened whipped cream.

White Hot Chocolate:

In saucepan, over medium heat, whisk:
    4 cups milk
    2 tablespoons sugar, until sugar is dissolved. Add:
    4 oz chopped white chocolate
    1 oz chopped milk chocolate
Remove from heat. Whisk until melted and frothy.
Top with: lightly sweetened whipped cream, white and dark chocolate shavings.

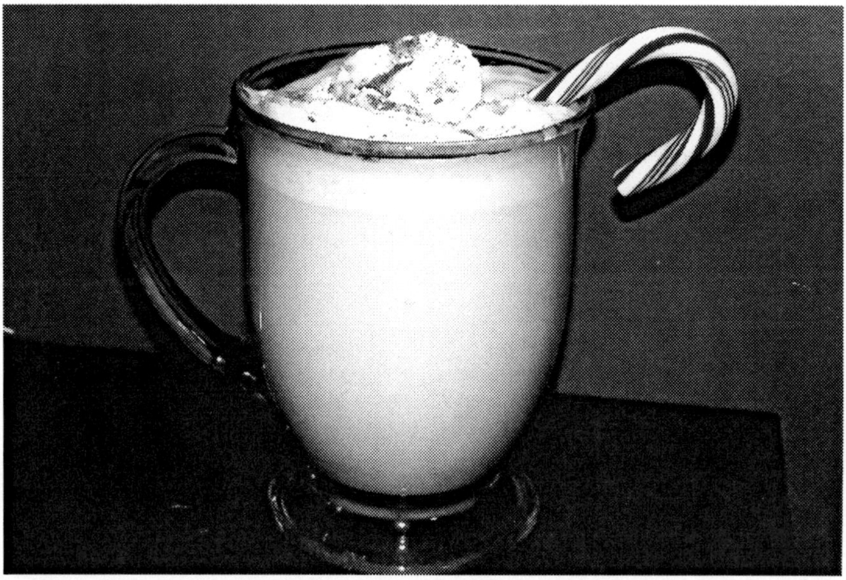

Coffee Cocktails

They say that alcohol is a slow poison. So, who's in a hurry?

Espresso martini:

Pour into a cocktail shaker:
    A double shot of cold espresso
    1½ oz vodka
    1 oz Kahlua
    ice
Shake and strain into a martini glass

Martini-ccino:

Pour into a cocktail shaker:
    A single shot of cold espresso
    ½ oz vanilla syrup
    1½ oz vodka
    1½ oz cream
    ice
Shake and strain into a martini glass, sprinkle with cocoa

Creamy Dreamy Martini:

Pour into a cocktail shaker!
    A double shot of cold espresso
    ½ oz Baileys

½ oz Frangelico
½ oz Tia Maria
2 oz milk
ice

Shake well. Serve in a tall glass with a straw.

Café Napoleon:

A cappuccino with 1 oz of Cognac garnished with whipped cream and chocolate shavings.

Café Yucatan:

A single shot of espresso with 1 oz of crème de cacao and topped with whipped cream, a sprinkle of nutmeg and grated orange zest.

Latte Royale:

A latte with 1½ oz of Frangelico hazelnut liqueur topped with whipped cream and a maraschino cherry.

Affogato:

Mix 1½ oz of Frangelico (or other liqueur) to a double shot of espresso. Add a scoop of vanilla ice cream.

Con Leche Shake:

Place in a blender:
 A double shot of espresso
 1½ tablespoons sweetened condensed milk
 ½ cup milk
 2 oz Kahlua or coffee liqueur
 A scoop of coffee ice cream

Blend until smooth. Serve in a tall glass garnished with whipped cream, a sprinkle of cocoa and chocolate covered espresso beans.

Coffee Cream Whiskey:

Place in a blender:
 ¼ cup cream
 ¼ cup sweetened condensed milk
 ½ cup bourbon

Have a Java

    1 shot espresso
    2 squirts chocolate syrup
    1 squirt vanilla syrup
    1 squirt almond syrup
Blend until smooth.

Biscottis

Perfect for dunking in your favorite coffee, not to mention the fact that they can keep in an airtight container at room temperature for up to two weeks–everyone loves biscottis.

Orange Cranberry Biscotti:

The unique texture comes from cornmeal. This one is my personal favorite and has developed a loyal fan club.
- 1¼ cups all purpose flour
- 1¼ cups yellow cornmeal
- ½ teaspoon baking powder
- ½ teaspoon salt
- 6 tablespoons butter, soft
- 1 cup sugar
- 2 large eggs
- 2 teaspoons pure orange extract
- 1 tablespoons grated orange zest
- 1 cup chopped almonds
- 1 cup dried cranberries
- 1 teaspoon anise seeds (fennel)

Preheat oven to 350° F.

In a bowl, combine flour, cornmeal, baking powder and salt. Set aside.

In bowl of electric mixer, cream the butter until smooth. Add the sugar and beat until fluffy. Add eggs, one at a time, beating well after each addition. Beat in orange extract.

Add the flour mixture to the butter mixture and beat on low speed until combined. Add orange zest, almonds, cranberries, anise seeds and beat until combined.

Transfer dough to a parchment paper lined baking sheet. Pat into a 14 x 3½ inch log. Bake 30 minutes, or until firm and slightly cracked on top. Remove from oven. Cool 15 minutes.

Transfer to a cutting board. With a serrated knife, cut the log crosswise into ½ inch slices. Return the slices to the baking sheet and bake for 18 minutes, rotating pan halfway through. Remove from oven and let cool completely on the baking sheet.

Makes 4 dozen

TRIPLE CHOCOLATE BISCOTTI:

This biscotti becomes the favorite of anyone in need of a quick chocolate fix.
    1¾ cups all purpose flour
    ⅓ cup cocoa
    2 teaspoons baking powder
    ½ teaspoon salt
    6 tablespoons butter, soft
    1 cup sugar
    3 large eggs
    1½ teaspoons vanilla extract
    8 oz semi sweet chocolate chips
    ½ cup white chocolate chips
Preheat oven to 350° F.

Line a baking sheet with two pieces of lightly greased tin foil. Sift together the flour, cocoa, baking powder and salt in a medium sized bowl.

In bowl of electric mixer, beat butter until creamy. Add sugar and beat until fluffy. Beat in eggs, one at a time, then vanilla. Add the flour mixture and beat on low speed until combined. Stir in the chocolate chips and the white chips.

Transfer dough to baking sheet. Shape into two 11x2½ inch logs. Refrigerate thirty minutes. Bake until logs are dry and cracked, about 25 minutes. Cool 10 minutes.

Reduce heat to 300° F. Lift logs by the first piece of tinfoil to a working surface. Cut the logs crosswise into ¾ inch slices. Return the slices to the baking sheet. Bake until just dry to the touch, about 8 minutes. Turn the slices over and bake for another 8 minutes. Remove from oven. Cool completely on baking sheet.
    Makes 3 dozen

ALMOND BISCOTTI:

The classic Italian biscotti.
    2 cups all purpose flour
    2 teaspoons baking powder
    ½ teaspoon salt
    ½ cup butter, soft
    1 cup sugar
    2 eggs
    ¼ cup amaretto liqueur
    1 teaspoon vanilla extract
    ½ cup chopped almonds
    1 tablespoon anise seeds (fennel seeds)
Preheat oven to 350° F. Grease and flour baking sheet.

In a bowl, combine the flour, baking powder and salt.

In bowl of electric mixer, cream the butter and sugar until light and fluffy. Add the eggs, one at a time. To this, add the dry ingredients alternately with the Amaretto. Add the vanilla and mix well. Fold in the almonds and anise seeds.

Turn dough onto lightly floured surface and form into a ball. Cut the ball in half. Form each half into a 12 x 2 inch log. Transfer logs to a baking sheet.

Bake 30 minutes. Remove from oven. Let cool 10 minutes.

Transfer to a cutting board and cut crosswise into ½ inch slices. Reduce heat to 300° F. Return slices to baking sheet and bake for 30 minutes, rotating sheet halfway through.

Cool completely on sheet.
    Makes 3 ½ dozen

ORANGE CHOCOLATE BISCOTTI:

The taste combination of orange and chocolate is addictive.
   3 cups all purpose flour
   2½ teaspoons baking powder
   ½ teaspoon salt
   ½ cup butter, soft
   ¾ cup sugar
   3 eggs, beaten
   1 teaspoon vanilla extract
   1 teaspoon orange extract
   1½ tablespoons orange rind, grated
   1 cup almonds, sliced, toasted
   1 cup chocolate chips
   2 tablespoons Amaretto liqueur
Preheat oven to 350° F.

With electric mixer, cream the butter until smooth. Add the sugar and beat until fluffy. Add orange rind, vanilla extract, orange extract.

Combine flour, baking powder and salt. Add to butter mixture and beat until smooth. Slowly add the beaten eggs. Add the Amaretto. Fold in the almonds and chocolate chips.

On lightly greased, parchment lined baking sheet, form dough into a 14 x 3½ inch log. Bake on lower rack of oven for 45 minutes. Remove from oven. Cool 10 minutes.

Cut loaf on the diagonal into slices ½ inch thick. Return slices to baking sheet and bake 15 minutes. Cool completely on baking sheet.
      Makes 4 dozen

CHOCOLATE PISTACHIO BISCOTTI:

A rich, dark, emerald studded biscotti.

    2 cups all purpose flour
    1 teaspoon baking powder
    ¼ teaspoon salt
    6 tablespoons butter, soft
    1 cup sugar
    2 large eggs
    1 cup pistachios, shelled
    ½ cup chocolate chips
    ½ cup unsweetened cocoa

Preheat oven to 350° F. Grease and flour a baking sheet.

In medium bowl, whisk flour, cocoa, baking soda and salt. In bowl of electric mixer, beat butter and sugar until fluffy. Add eggs, beating after each addition. Add dry ingredients and beat until a stiff dough is formed. Fold in pistachios and chocolate chips.

Transfer to baking sheet and form dough into a 12 x 4 inch log. Bake 25 minutes or until firm to the touch. Cool 10 minutes. Reduce heat to 300° F.

Transfer log onto a cutting board and cut crosswise into 1 inch slices. Arrange on baking sheet and bake 10 minutes.

        Makes 3 dozen

Biscottis 25

Scones

Rich, tender, buttery scones are the perfect companion to any pot of hot tea. They are surprisingly easy and quick to make at home. Really, the only thing you have to remember if you want a high rise, flaky scone, is that the butter must be cold–and I mean cold! I suggest putting the butter into your freezer for 15 minutes before using it in your recipe.

They are wonderful on their own or serve them with clotted cream, jam or flavored butter.

BLUEBERRY SCONES:

They are equally delicious made with raspberries.

- 2 cups all purpose flour
- 3 tablespoons brown sugar
- ½ teaspoon baking soda
- 2 teaspoons baking powder
- ½ teaspoon salt
- ½ cup cold butter
- 1 cup blueberries, fresh or frozen
- 1 cup sour cream
- 1 large egg yolk, beaten
- 1 large egg white, beaten
- 1 tablespoon water
- 1 tablespoon coarse sugar

Preheat oven to 425° F.

Stir together flour, brown sugar, baking powder, baking soda and salt in a large bowl. With pastry blender or two knives, cut in butter until mixture resembles coarse crumbs. Add blueberries and toss to mix.

In a small bowl, combine sour cream and egg yolk. Add to flour–butter mixture and stir with a fork just until moistened. Turn onto a lightly floured surface, knead a few times to mix. Divide dough in half. Pat each half into a circle ¾ inch thick. Cut each circle into 6 wedges. Brush tops with the egg white mixed with the water. Sprinkle with coarse sugar. Place 1 inch apart on a slightly greased baking sheet.

Bake 15-18 minutes, rotating pan halfway through. Cool on wire rack for 10 minutes.
        Makes 12 scones

APPLE DATE SCONES:

These scones are both healthy and scrumptious.
    1½ cups all purpose flour
    ½ cup whole wheat flour
    ¼ cup brown sugar
    ¼ cup bran
    ½ teaspoon baking soda
    2 teaspoon baking powder
    1 teaspoon salt
    ½ cup cold butter
    1 egg
    2 tablespoons cinnamon
    ²/₃ cup buttermilk
    ²/₃ cup chopped dates
    ²/₃ cup chopped granny smith apples
Preheat oven to 400° F.

Stir together flours, bran, baking powder, baking soda, salt, cinnamon and brown sugar in a large bowl. With pastry blender or two knives, cut in butter until mixture resembles coarse crumbs.

In a small bowl, whisk egg and buttermilk. Add to flour–butter mixture. Stir with a fork until just combined. Add dates and apples. Turn onto a lightly floured surface, knead a few times to mix. Divide dough in half. Pat each half into a circle ¾ inch thick. Cut each circle into 6 wedges. Place 1 inch apart on slightly greased baking sheet.

Bake 15-18 minutes, rotating pan halfway through. Remove from oven and sprinkle the tops of scones with coarse sugar, if desired. Cool on wire rack for 10 minutes.
    Makes 12 scones

ORANGE CHOCOLATE CHIP SCONES:

The orange glaze keeps these scones flavorful and moist
- 1¾ cups all purpose flour
- ½ cup whole wheat flour
- ⅓ cup sugar
- 2 teaspoons baking powder
- ½ teaspoon salt
- 5 tablespoons cold butter
- ½ cup chocolate chips
- 3 tablespoons orange juice

Preheat oven to 400° F.

In a large bowl, stir together flour, baking powder, salt and sugar. Using two knives, cut in butter until mixture is crumbly. Add the chocolate chips and orange juice. Mix with a fork just until moistened.

Turn the dough onto a lightly floured surface and knead quickly a few times to mix well. Pat into a 9 inch circle. Cut into 8 wedges, Place 1 inch apart on lightly greased baking sheet. Bake 15 minutes, rotating pan halfway through. Remove from oven. Cool 10 minutes on sheet then brush with orange glaze.

Makes 8 scones.

Orange Glaze:

- 1 cup icing sugar
- 2-4 tbsp orange juice

Add the orange juice to the icing sugar until it is a good drizzling consistency.

OATMEAL SCONES:

This is the best way to eat your oatmeal for breakfast.
    1¼ cups all purpose flour
    1/3 cup sugar
    2 teaspoon baking powder
    ½ teaspoon salt
    ½ cup cold butter
    ¼ cup raisins
    1 egg
    1/3 cup buttermilk
    1 cup rolled oats, old fashioned
    cream and coarse sugar for tops of scones
Preheat oven to 375° F.

Mix the flour, sugar, baking powder and salt in a large bowl. With two knives or a pastry blender, cut in the butter until crumbly. Add the oats and the raisins.

In a small bowl, whisk the egg with the buttermilk. Add all at once to the flour–butter mixture and stir just until combined. Turn onto a lightly floured surface and pat into a 9 inch circle. Cut until 8 wedges. Brush with the cream and sprinkle with coarse sugar. Place 1 inch apart on a lightly greased baking sheet and bake 15 minutes, rotating pan halfway through.
    Makes 8 scones.

Tip: Never use instant oats for baking since they absorb water immediately and the cooking process will turn your baked goods into cement.

RAISIN SCONES:

You can't go wrong with this high tea classic.
    2 cups all purpose flour
    2 tablespoon sugar
    1 teaspoon baking powder
    1 teaspoon salt
    ½ cup cold butter
    1 cup sour cream
    ¾ cup raisins
    2 eggs
    1 tablespoon flour
    cream and coarse sugar for tops of scones
Preheat oven to 400° F.

Combine flour, sugar, baking powder, and salt in the bowl of an electric mixer. Add the butter, cubed and blend on low until the mixture resembles coarse crumbs.

In a small bowl, combine the eggs with the sour cream. Add to the flour mixture and combine just until blended. Coat the raisins with the flour and add to the dough. Mix quickly.

Transfer the dough to a floured surface and pat into a 9 x 6 inch square about 1¼ inches thick. Using a floured knife, cut into four 3 inch squares. Cut squares in half on the diagonal to form 8 triangles. Transfer to a lightly greased baking sheet and brush tops with the cream then sprinkle with the sugar. Bake 20-25 minutes, rotating pan halfway through.
    Makes 8 scones.

MAPLE SYRUP BUTTER:

Delicious with absolutely everything:
    1 cup butter, soft
    ½ cup maple syrup
    4 Tablespoons honey
    Beat together until smooth and creamy.

MUFFINS

Have you ever noticed the way that muffins keep reinventing themselves all day long? They start off as breakfast, turn into an afternoon snack and finally transmogrify into dessert.

The following recipes are for our five most popular muffins. If made in regular muffin tins, you'll get twelve muffins. We use the jumbo muffin tins to get 6 to 8 giant muffins. (Most people agree that bigger is better in the muffin world.)

Fill the muffin tins three quarters full with the batter because if you overfill them, your muffins will have flat tops instead of rounded ones. Aesthetics aside, they will still be delicious.

LEMON POPPYSEED MUFFINS:
These could also be called "Dental Floss Muffins" but you'll smile anyways.
    1¾ cups all purpose flour
    ¾ cup sugar
    2 teaspoon baking powder
    ¼ teaspoon salt
    1¼ teaspoons baking soda
    1 egg
    ¾ cup buttermilk
    ¼ cup fresh lemon juice
    ½ cup melted butter

1 tablespoon poppy seeds
1 tablespoon lemon zest, finely grated
Preheat oven to 350° F.

    Combine flour, sugar, baking powder, baking soda and salt in a large mixing bowl. Make a well in the center.

    In separate bowl, whisk the egg, buttermilk and lemon juice. Add to the dry ingredients, stirring just until combined. Stir in the melted butter, but don't over mix. Stir in the poppy seeds and lemon zest. Spoon in greased muffin pans and bake for 20-22 minutes, or until golden.

    Sprinkle with raw sugar when removing from oven, if desired.
        Makes 12 muffins

RHUBARB MUFFINS:

If you love rhubarb the way I do–this one's for you.
- 1½ cups brown sugar
- ¼ cup oil
- 2 eggs
- 2 teaspoons vanilla extract
- 1 cup buttermilk
- 1½ cups rhubarb, finely diced
- ½ cup chopped nuts
- 2½ cups all purpose flour
- 1 teaspoon baking powder
- 1 teaspoon baking soda
- ½ teaspoon salt

Topping:

- ⅓ cup sugar
- 1½ teaspoons cinnamon
- 1 tablespoon butter, melted

Preheat oven to 425° F.

Combine flour, baking powder, baking soda and salt in a medium size bowl.

In a large bowl, whisk the brown sugar, oil, eggs, vanilla, buttermilk and rhubarb. Add dry ingredients, stirring just until blended. Fold in nuts. Spoon into greased muffin pans.

Combine the topping ingredients in a small bowl and sprinkle over muffins.

Bake 20 minutes or until they test done. *
Makes 12 muffins.

* They are done when a toothpick inserted in the center comes out clean.

TRIPLE CHOCOLATE MUFFINS:

I like to stud these beauties with a couple of white chocolate chips as soon as they come out of the oven for the black and white color contrast. The taste doesn't need any help.

    1 ¼ cups all purpose flour
    ½ cup cocoa
    ½ teaspoon baking powder
    ½ teaspoon baking soda
    ½ teaspoon salt
    2 eggs
    4 tablespoons butter, melted
    ¾ cup sugar
    ¾ cup milk
    1 tablespoon vegetable oil
    2 teaspoons vanilla extract
    1 cup dark chocolate chips
    ½ cup white chocolate chips

Preheat oven to 350° F.

In bowl, whisk together flour, cocoa, baking powder, baking soda, salt.

In another bowl, beat the eggs then whisk in the melted butter. Beat in the sugar, milk, vegetable oil and vanilla.

Stir the wet ingredients into the dry ingredients. Fold in the dark and white chocolate chips. Spoon batter into paper lined, greased muffin pans.

Bake 20 minutes or until they test done.
        Makes 12 muffins.

TROPICAL CARROT MUFFINS:

These are always the first muffins to sell out and we make twice as many as the others. Try them and you'll understand why.

    1½ cups all purpose flour
    ⅔ cup sugar
    1 teaspoon baking soda
    1 teaspoon baking powder
    ½ teaspoon salt
    1 teaspoon cinnamon
    ¼ teaspoon nutmeg
    ⅔ cup vegetable oil
    2 eggs
    1 cup carrots, shredded
    1 teaspoon vanilla extract
    ½ cup sweetened coconut, shredded
    ¼ cup raisins
    ½ cup chopped nuts (optional)

Preheat oven to 350° F.

Sift together the flour, sugar, baking soda, baking powder, salt, cinnamon and nutmeg. Make a well in the center.

In separate bowl combine all the other ingredients. Add to the dry ingredients and stir just until combined. Spoon into greased muffin pans and sprinkle some chopped nuts over tops for decoration. Bake for 25 minutes or until they test done.

    Makes 12 muffins.

CRANBERRY ORANGE MUFFINS:

You can keep the orange cranberry sauce in your fridge and mix up the dry ingredients before going to bed. Simply assemble everything in the morning and 20 minutes later you have great muffins, fresh from the oven.

   2 cups whole wheat flour
   1 cup natural bran
   ½ cup sugar
   1 teaspoon baking powder
   1 teaspoon baking soda
   2 eggs
   ½ cup butter, melted

Orange-Cranberry Sauce:

   1 package fresh or frozen cranberries
   1 cup sugar
   1 cup water
   grated zest of 2 oranges

Preheat oven to 375° F.

In a medium saucepan, combine all the ingredients for the orange-cranberry sauce. Bring to a boil then simmer, stirring occasionally until thickened, about 10 minutes. Remove from heat and let cool.

Combine flour, bran, sugar, baking powder and baking soda.

In separate bowl, beat eggs, melted butter and 1½ cups orange-cranberry sauce. Add dry ingredients, stirring just until blended. Spoon into greased muffin pans. Top with a cranberry for decoration.

Bake 15-20 minutes or until they test done.
         Makes 12 muffins.

OATMEAL DATE MUFFINS:

When our customers begrudgingly opt for this muffin instead of a chocolate one, they don't regret it.
 1 cup all purpose flour
 ½ cup sugar
 1½ teaspoon baking powder
 1 teaspoon salt
 ½ teaspoon baking soda
 1⅓ cup rolled oats–old fashioned
 1 cup chopped dates
 1 cup buttermilk
 ¼ cup butter, melted and cooled
 ¼ cup molasses
 1 egg, beaten
Preheat oven to 400° F.

Combine flour, sugar, baking powder, salt and baking soda. Mix in the rolled oats and the dates.

In separate bowl, whisk together buttermilk, cooled butter, molasses and egg. Add to the dry ingredients and beat just until moistened. Spoon into greased muffin pans and bake 25 minutes or until they test done. Sprinkle with raw sugar when removing from oven, if desired.

 Makes 12 muffins

Tip: When I rotate my pans halfway through the baking time–which is a good idea for all baked goods–I decorate the tops with a sliver of date. If I do so before putting them in the oven, I risk having them sink into the muffins while they are cooking.

BLUEBERRY MUFFINS:

As with the blueberry scones, you could just as successfully use frozen raspberries.
    3 cups all purpose flour
    ¾ cup sugar
    1½ tablespoons baking powder
    ¾ teaspoon salt
    1½ cups buttermilk
    6 tbsp butter, melted, slightly cooled
    1½ teaspoons vanilla extract
    1½ cups blueberries, fresh or frozen.
Preheat oven to 350° F.

In large mixing bowl combine flour, sugar, baking powder and salt.

In separate bowl whisk the buttermilk, melted butter and vanilla. Add to the flour mixture and stir until just combined. Fold in the blueberries. Spoon batter into greased muffin pans. Bake 20-22 minutes.
    Makes 12 muffins.

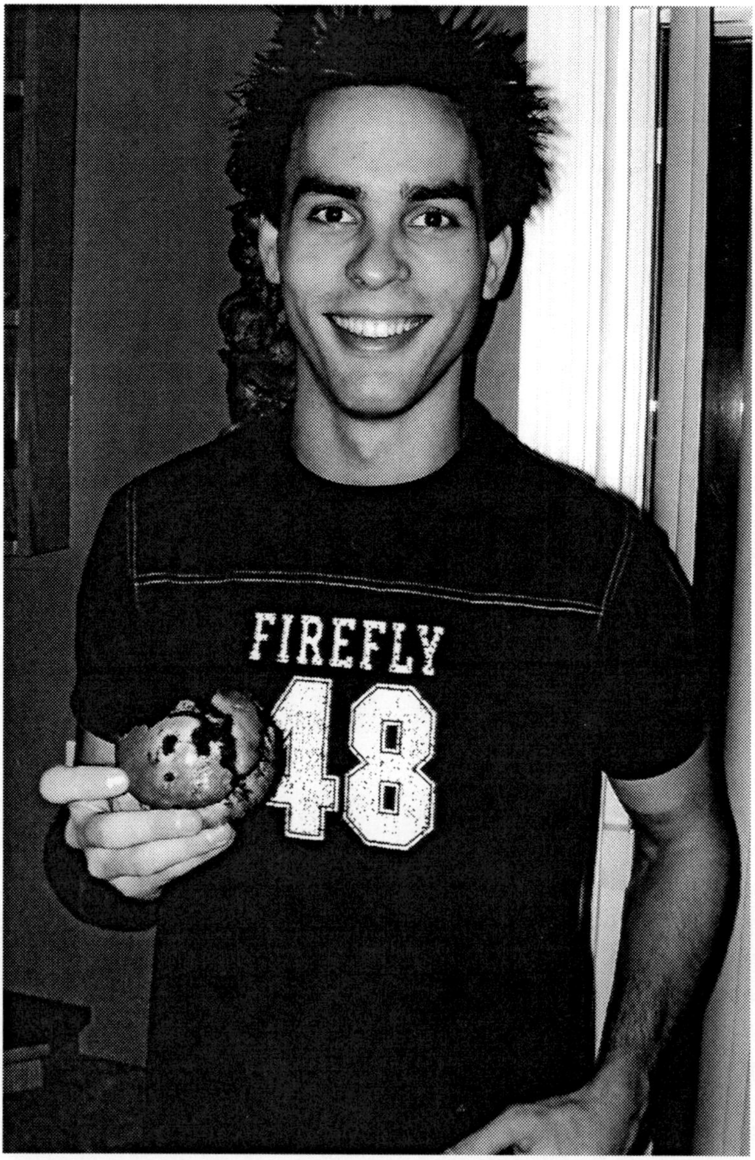
FIREFLY
48

Sweet Loaf Breads

Not technically bread, not muffins, not cake–these loaves are a combination of all three. They can be sliced and buttered like a loaf of bread, eaten "as-is" like a muffin or iced like a cake. The only thing they can't be–is resisted!

BANANA BREAD:

Only the very strong can turn their backs on this wonderfully tender bread fresh out of the oven.

    3 cups all purpose flour
    1½ teaspoons baking soda
    1½ teaspoons baking powder
    2 cups sugar
    1 cup butter, soft
    2 eggs
    1 cup buttermilk
    4 bananas, mashed
    1 teaspoon vanilla extract

Preheat oven to 350° F.

    In bowl, sift flour, baking soda and baking powder. In separate bowl, with an electric mixer, cream the butter and the sugar together. Add the eggs, beating well after each addition. Add the vanilla. Mash the bananas into the buttermilk. Add the flour mixture to the butter mixture alternately with the buttermilk.

Pour into two greased and floured 6 x 4 inch loaf pans. Bake 1 hour or until they test done.

Makes 2 loaves.

CARROT BREAD:

The slow oven makes this bread *so* moist.

   1 cup sugar
   1 cup vegetable oil
   3 eggs, beaten
   1 1/3 cups all purpose flour
   1 1/3 teaspoons baking powder
   1 1/3 teaspoons baking soda
   1 1/3 teaspoons cinnamon
   ½ teaspoon salt
   ¾ cup raisins
   ½ cup crushed pineapple
   ¾ cup nuts, chopped
   ½ cup coconut, sweetened, flaked
   2 cups carrots, shredded

Preheat oven to 300° F.

Whisk up the sugar, oil and eggs. In a large bowl, sift together the flour, baking powder, baking soda, cinnamon and salt. Add the sugar mixture and mix well. Add the raisins, pineapple, nuts, coconut and carrots. Pour into a greased floured 9 x 5 inch load pan. Bake for 1 hour 15 minutes. Remove from oven and cool on wire rack.

Carrot cake: If desired, pour batter in a greased, floured tube pan and bake 1 hour 15 minutes. Cool slightly, remove from pan and ice with cream cheese icing when completely cool.

          Makes 1 loaf

Cream Cheese Icing:

   4 oz cream cheese
   4 oz butter, soft
   2 tsp vanilla extract
   2 cups icing sugar

With mixer, cream together the cream cheese, butter and vanilla until light and fluffy. Slowly beat in the icing sugar until well incorporated and smooth.

LEMON NUT BREAD:

The sweet-tart taste makes this bread a real sweetheart.
- 1½ cups all purpose flour
- 1 teaspoon baking powder
- 1½ teaspoons salt
- 1 teaspoon lemon zest, grated
- ½ cup vegetable shortening
- ¾ cup sugar
- 2 eggs
- ½ cup milk
- ½ cup nuts, chopped

Preheat oven to 350° F.

In bowl, mix flour, baking powder, salt and zest. In large mixing bowl, cream the shortening and the sugar with an electric mixer. Add the eggs, one at a time, beating well after each addition. Add the dry ingredients to the shortening mixture alternately with the milk, mixing well. Fold in the nuts. Pour into a 9 x 5 inch greased loaf pan. Bake about 1 hour or until it tests done.

Let the bread rest in the pan 15 minutes. Pierce holes in the bread with a toothpick and spoon the lemon glaze all over. Remove from pan after 10 minutes.

Makes 1 loaf

Lemon glaze:

- ¼ cup lemon juice
- 1 tbsp corn syrup
- 2 tbsp sugar

Place all ingredients in a saucepan. Stir over medium heat until sugar is melted. Let syrup cool slightly before using.

FINANCIER:

These little almond cakes, the kind you see in a Parisian Café, are meltingly delicate and deceptively easy to make.

  1 cup all purpose flour
  1 cup ground almonds
  1 1/3 cups icing sugar
  2-3 tablespoons vanilla sugar
  pinch of salt
  8 egg whites
  2/3 cup butter, melted
  sliced almonds for garnishing
  icing sugar, for dusting

Preheat oven to 400° F.

With cooking spray, grease 15 tins 4 x 2 inches (if you prefer, you can use three mini loaf pans 5 x 3 inches each or even mini muffin pans).

In a large bowl, sift flour, ground almonds, icing sugar and vanilla sugar. Mix thoroughly.

In separate bowl, with electric mixer, add the salt to the egg whites and whip up until very stiff. Fold this mixture carefully into the flour mixture. Quickly fold in the melted butter.

Divide the batter between the baking tins and sprinkle the tops with some sliced almonds.

Bake 15-20 minutes until they test done but being careful not to over bake. Dust with icing sugar when they have cooled completely.

  Makes 16 cakes

Vanilla Sugar:

  ½ vanilla bean, split lengthwise
  2 cups sugar

Scrape seeds of vanilla bean into a bowl and stir in sugar until well combined. Store in an airtight container up to 1 month.

IRISH CREAM POUND CAKE:

More cake than loaf but so deliciously decadent I just had to include it.
- 4 cup all purpose flour
- 1½ cups butter, soft
- 3 cups sugar
- 6 large eggs
- 1½ teaspoons instant coffee granules
- ¼ cup boiling water
- ½ cup Irish cream liqueur
- 1 teaspoon vanilla extract
- 1 teaspoon almond extract

Preheat oven to 300° F.

In bowl of electric mixer, beat the butter until creamy. Gradually add the sugar and beat 7 minutes. Add the eggs, one at a time, beating until the yellow has disappeared.

In small bowl dissolve the instant coffee in boiling waiter. Stir in the Irish cream liquor. Add this mixture, alternating with the flour, to the butter mixture on low speed until just blended. Stir in vanilla and almond extracts.

Pour batter into a greased, floured tube pan and bake 1 hour 40 minutes or until it tests done.

Makes 1 cake

Irish Cream Glaze:

- 1½ cups icing sugar
- ⅛ cup Irish Cream liqueur

Mix well. Drizzle over cooled cake. Top with toasted, sliced almonds.

CINNAMON BUNS:

Yummy sticky goodness that no self respecting Coffee House would be without.

For the dough;

    4 cups all purpose flour
    2 teaspoons yeast
    2 tablespoons sugar
    1 teaspoon salt
    ½ cup butter, soft
    2 eggs
    1¼ cups milk, lukewarm

Preheat oven to 350° F.

In bowl, mix flour, yeast, sugar, and salt. Add the butter, eggs, and milk. Stir to combine then knead dough into a ball. Knead dough for 5 minutes either with your hands or the dough hook of electric mixer. Place dough in a large, greased bowl. Turn dough over. Cover dough with a clean cloth and let rise in a warm, dry place for 45 minutes.

For the filling;

    1 tablespoon butter, melted
    ½ cup brown sugar
    1 teaspoon ground cinnamon

Mix together the brown sugar and cinnamon. Roll the dough on floured surface into a 20 x 14 inch rectangle. Brush with melted butter. Sprinkle the brown sugar filling over surface of dough. Roll the dough away from you by the long end as if making a cake roll. Cut into 10 slices. Place slices in a buttered 15 x 10 inch glass baking dish. Let rise in a warm place 1½ hours.

Bake for 25 minutes. When removing from oven, scatter 1 cup roasted pecans over the top. Cool 10-15 minutes then drizzle the icing over the buns.

        Makes 10 cinnamon buns

Caramel Icing:

    ¼ cup butter

¼ cup corn syrup
½ cup brown sugar
2 tablespoons water
Place all in saucepan and heat, stirring, until melted and homogeneous.

Cookies

All of these cookies are winners and can call your name from clear across the room. Chocolate seems to have the loudest voice of all. Even so, the oatmeal, sugar and peanut butter have developed a fiercely loyal following. We make sure to always be well stocked with chocolate macaroons because they sell out quickly. Make them and you'll know why.

PEANUT BUTTER OATMEAL COOKIES:

As a lover of all things peanut butter–let me tell you–this is one good cookie.

½ cup butter, soft
1 cup creamy peanut butter
½ cup light brown sugar
½ cup white sugar
1 teaspoon baking powder
½ teaspoon baking soda
1 large egg
1 teaspoon vanilla extract
1 cup all purpose flour
1 cup oats, quick cooking
peanuts for decorating

Preheat oven to 350° F.

In bowl of electric mixer, beat butter and peanut butter until smooth. Add sugars, baking powder and baking soda and beat until light and fluffy. Beat in egg and vanilla. On low speed, beat in flour and oats.

Roll into 2 inch balls. Place 2 inches apart on parchment lined baking sheets. Flatten slightly with a fork and press a peanut in the middle of each cookie.

Bake 10-12 minutes, rotating pans halfway through. Cool on sheets one minute then transfer to wire rack to cool completely.
    Makes 4 dozen

WHITE CHOCOLATE, COCONUT AND MACADAMIA COOKIES:

Omit the coconut if you don't want any–but why wouldn't you want any?
    2½ cups all purpose flour
    1 teaspoon baking soda
    ½ teaspoon salt
    1 cup butter, soft
    ⅔ cup white sugar
    ⅔ cup brown sugar
    1 large egg
    2 tablespoon milk
    1½ teaspoons vanilla extract
    ¾ cup white chocolate, chopped
    1 cup coconut, sweetened, shredded
    1 cup macadamia nuts, chopped
Preheat oven to 350° F.

Sift together the flour, baking soda and salt. With an electric mixer, cream the butter until fluffy. Add the sugars and beat 3 minutes more. Add the egg, then the milk and vanilla. Fold in the white chocolate, coconut and macadamia nuts.

Drop by tablespoonfuls onto ungreased baking sheets. Bake 10-12 minutes, rotating pans halfway through. Cool a few minutes on pans then transfer to wire rack to cool completely.
        Makes 3 dozen

CHOCOLATE GINGER COOKIES:

The chewy texture and fresh ginger gives this cookie a bite that will make everyone want to bite back.

    1½ cups all purpose flour
    1¼ teaspoons ground ginger
    1 teaspoon cinnamon
    ¼ teaspoon ground cloves
    ¼ teaspoon ground nutmeg
    1 tablespoon cocoa
    ½ cup butter, soft
    1 tablespoon fresh ginger, grated
    ½ cup brown sugar
    ½ cup molasses
    1 teaspoon baking soda
    1½ teaspoons boiling water
    ¾ cup chocolate chips
    sugar for rolling

Preheat oven to 350° F.

Sift together flour, ginger, cinnamon, cloves, nutmeg and cocoa.

In bowl of electric mixer, beat the butter and fresh ginger until light and fluffy, about 4 minutes. Beat in brown sugar then molasses.

In small bowl, dissolve baking soda in boiling water. Add half the flour mixture to the creamed mixture and beat until combined. Mix in the baking soda water then beat in the remaining flour mixture. Fold in the chocolate chips. Refrigerate the dough at least 2 hours.

Form dough into 2 inch balls. Roll in sugar and place 2 inches apart on two parchment lined baking sheets. Bake 10-12 minutes or until the surface cracks slightly, rotating pans halfway through. Cool 5 minutes on sheets then transfer to wire racks to cool completely.

        Makes 1½ dozen

CLASSIC CHOCOLATE CHIP COOKIES:

For a soft and chewy cookie, use butter and eggs right out of the fridge.
- 1½ cups all purpose flour
- 1½ teaspoons baking soda
- ½ teaspoon salt
- ⅔ cup butter, cold
- ½ cup sugar
- ½ cup brown sugar
- 1 egg, cold
- 1 teaspoon vanilla extract
- 1 cup semisweet chocolate chips

Preheat oven to 350° F.

Sift together the flour, baking soda and salt. In bowl of electric mixer, cream the butter until light and fluffy then continue beating 3 minutes more. Beat in egg then vanilla. Add the flour mixture and beat until combined. Fold in the chocolate chips. Drop by rounded teaspoonfuls, 2 inches apart, on ungreased baking sheets.

Bake 10-12 minutes, rotating pans halfway through. Cool a few minutes on sheets then transfer to wire racks to cool completely.

Makes 2 ½ dozen

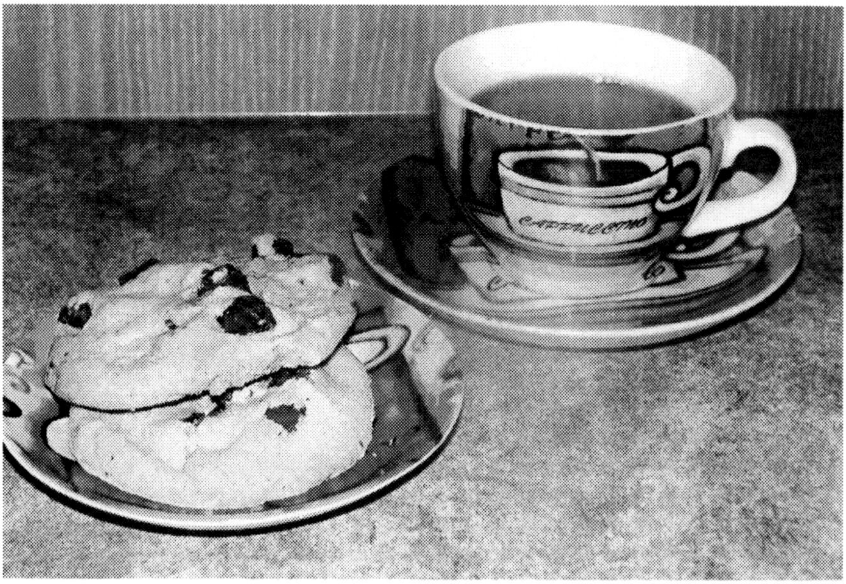

OATMEAL RAISIN COOKIES:

Not everyone loves raisins so you can omit them or replace them by chocolate chips.
- 1½ cups all purpose flour
- 1 teaspoon cinnamon
- 1 teaspoon baking soda
- 1 teaspoon salt
- 1 cup coconut, sweetened, shredded
- 1 cup butter, soft
- 1 cup brown sugar
- 1/3 cup maple syrup
- 1 egg, large
- 2 teaspoons vanilla extract
- 3 cups rolled oats, old fashioned

Preheat oven to 350° F.

Sift the flour, cinnamon, baking soda and salt together. Stir in the coconut.

With electric mixer beat the butter and brown sugar until light and fluffy. Continue beating for 3 minutes. Beat in the maple syrup, egg and vanilla. Beat 1 minute more. Add the dry ingredients and beat just until combined. Add the oats and raisins.

Drop by rounded spoonfuls onto parchment lined baking sheets. Bake 10 minutes, rotating pans halfway through. Cool a few minutes on sheets then transfer to wire racks to cool completely.

Makes 3 dozen

SUGAR COOKIES:

Absolutely melts in your mouth. You'll wonder if it's a cookie or soft ice cream.
- 1 cup butter
- 1 teaspoon vanilla
- ¾ cup sugar
- 2 eggs
- 2 cups all purpose flour
- 1 teaspoon cream of tartar
- ½ teaspoon baking soda
- ¼ teaspoon nutmeg
- ¼ teaspoon salt

Preheat oven to 350° F.

Sift together the flour, cream of tartar, baking soda, nutmeg and salt.

Beat the butter and vanilla together in bowl of electric mixer for several minutes. Gradually add the sugar and beat 1 minute more. Add the eggs, one at a time, beating well after each addition. Gradually mix in the dry ingredients and beat for 1 minute.

Drop by tablespoonfuls onto lightly greased baking sheets. Bake 6-8 minutes. Sprinkle with sugar while still warm for a sparkly effect. Cool a few minutes on the sheets then transfer to wire racks to cool completely.

Makes 2 dozen

CHOCOLATE MACAROONS:

There's only one way to introduce these chocolately-luscious, made in the microwave, macaroons–Ta Dah!

    3½ cups oats, quick cook
    1 cup coconut, sweetened, shredded
    ½ cup walnuts, finely chopped
    ½ cup butter
    2 cups sugar
    ½ cup cocoa
    ¾ cup evaporated milk–not 2%
    ½ teaspoon vanilla

In an 8 cup ovenproof glass bowl, melt the butter at high for 1 minute. Blend in the cocoa. Pour in the evaporated milk and mix well. Microwave on high, uncovered, for 2 minutes. Stir and continue to microwave on high for 2½ to 3 minutes or until mixture has come to a full, rolling boil for 1 minute.

Stir in vanilla and dry ingredients. Mix well. Using two teaspoons, drop onto wax paper and sprinkle with more shredded coconut, if desired.

Let mounds stand 3-4 hours at room temperature until firm.
    Makes 3 dozen

Squares and Bars

From the ever popular brownie to the grown up date square, these sweets aren't only for special occasions. Rather, they make any occasion special.

GOOEY FUDGEY PEANUT BUTTER BROWNIES:

Using a cake mix for the base makes these brownies easy–everything else we use makes them irresistible.

Base;

¼ cup sweetened condensed milk
½ cup butter, melted and cooled
¼ cup milk
1 (18.25 oz) package 'Devil's Food Cake Mix'
1 egg
½ cup nuts, chopped

Topping;

½ cup sweetened condensed milk
1 (7 oz) jar marshmallow cream (1¾ cups)
½ cup peanut butter chips

Preheat oven to 350° F.

Combine ¼ cup condensed milk, butter, milk, cake mix, egg and nuts. Press two thirds of batter into a greased 13 x 9 inch baking pan. Bake 10 minutes.

In bowl, combine ½ cup condensed milk with marshmallow cream. Stir in the peanut butter chips. Spread this mixture evenly over brownie layer. Carefully spoon the remaining batter, by spoonfuls, over marshmallow mixture. Bake for 30 minutes. Cool completely.

Makes 2 dozen

BLONDIES:

With two brownie recipes, I couldn't let this beautiful blonde feel slighted. They also freeze well to become ice princesses.

1 cup all purpose flour
1½ teaspoons baking powder
1 cup butter, melted
1½ cups packed dark brown sugar
2 large eggs
1 teaspoon vanilla extract
½ cup white chocolate chips
½ cup butterscotch chips
²/₃ cup macadamia nuts, chopped

Preheat oven to 350° F.

In bowl, mix flour and baking powder. Set aside. In separate bowl, cream the butter and brown sugar with the electric mixer. Add the eggs and vanilla extract until creamy. Add the flour mixture and when incorporated add the chips and nuts.

Pour into a 13 x 9 inch greased baking pan. Bake 20-25 minutes. Cool completely before cutting into squares.

Makes 24 squares

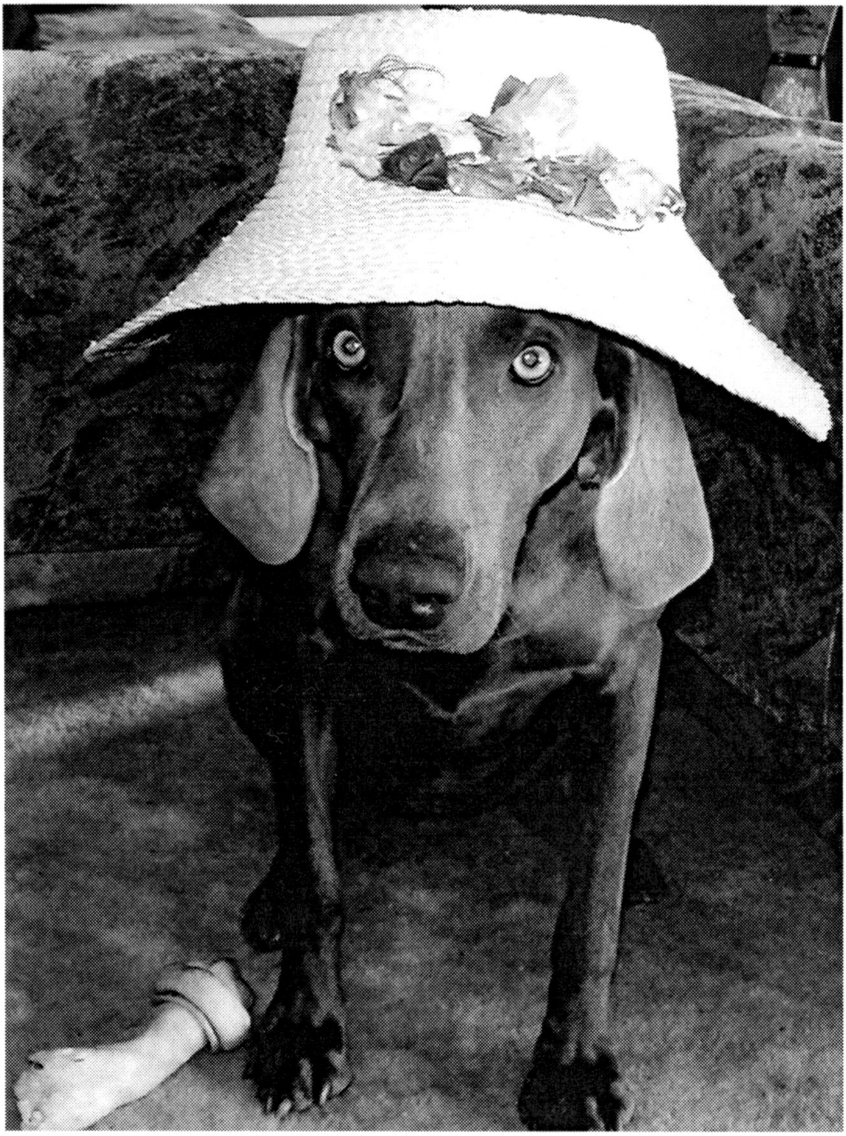

CHOCOLATE PEANUT BUTTER SQUARES:

For all of us who love those chocolate–peanut butter cups.
- 1½ cups icing sugar
- 1 cup graham cracker crumbs
- ½ cup peanut butter
- ½ cup butter
- 1 cup semisweet chocolate chips

Mix icing sugar and graham cracker crumbs. Melt the peanut butter and butter in microwave until smooth. Stir into crumb mixture. Press into an un-greased 8 x 8 inch pan.

Melt chocolate chips in microwave or over a pot of simmering water until smooth. Spread over the crumb mixture in the pan. Refrigerate at least 30 minutes. Cut into squares with a knife dipped in hot water.

        Makes 12 squares

DATE SQUARES:

The sweet that goes so well with your afternoon coffee and a good book.

   2 cups dates
   1 cup orange juice
   ¾ cup butter, soft
   2/3 cup brown sugar
   1 cup whole wheat flour
   2 cups rolled oats, old fashioned

Preheat oven to 350° F.

Put dates and orange juice in a saucepan. Cover and simmer over med-low heat, stirring occasionally.

In bowl of electric mixer, cream butter and brown sugar. Stir in the flour then the oats. Press 2/3 of this mixture into an 8 x 8 inch pan.

Spread the date filling over mixture in pan then top with remaining flour mixture. Bake 25-30 minutes, rotating pan halfway through.

       Makes 12 squares

BUTTER BARS:

The title sounds like these should be illegal; but you know–all things in moderation ... I dare you!

Base;

    1½ cups all purpose flour
    ½ cup brown sugar
    ½ cup butter, soft

Filling;

    4 eggs
    2 teaspoons vanilla
    $2/3$ cup sugar
    ½ cup all purpose flour
    ¼ teaspoon salt
    $2/3$ cup corn syrup
    1½ cups golden raisins

Preheat oven to 350° F.

Base:

Grease 13 x 9 inch baking pan. In bowl, beat butter and brown sugar until creamy. Stir in flour. Press into bottom of baking pan. Bake 12 minutes or until golden.

Filling:

In bowl, whisk eggs with vanilla and salt. Beat in sugar. Whisk in ½ cup flour, gradually. Stir in corn syrup until mixed then add raisins. Pour over base.

    Bake 20-25 minutes. Cool at least 3 hours before cutting into squares.
          Makes 24 squares

OAT CAKES:

Put a basket of these little gems on the breakfast table. Any leftovers will be nibbled on all day.

½ teaspoon baking soda
½ cup boiling water
1¼ cups sugar
2 cups rolled oats
2 cups all purpose flour
1 teaspoon baking powder
1 teaspoon salt
2 cups bran flakes type cereal
1 cup coconut, sweetened, shredded
1½ cups shortening

Preheat oven to 350° F.

Dissolve the baking soda in the boiling water. In a large bowl, combine the sugar, oats, flour, baking powder, salt, bran flakes and coconut. Cut in the shortening until mixture resembles coarse crumbs. Stir in soda-water.

Pat the batter into a greased 13 x 9 inch baking pan. Bake 15 minutes or until golden.

Makes 12 oatcakes

Squares and Bars 67

TRIPLE CHOCOLATE BROWNIES:

So beautiful with the ribbons of chocolate and white chocolate butter-cream frosting but the truth is—these brownies are so good they don't need the frosting at all.

    1½ cups butter
    1 1/3 cups cocoa
    2½ cups sugar
    ½ teaspoon salt
    2 teaspoons vanilla extract
    6 eggs, beaten
    1 1/3 cups cake flour
    1 cup chocolate chips or chunks

Preheat oven to 350° F.

Grease two 9 x 9 inch pans. In saucepan, melt the butter. Remove from heat and whisk in the cocoa. Set aside to cool completely.

Combine the sugar, salt and vanilla in the chocolate mixture. Beat in the eggs then fold in the flour until just combined. Fold in the chocolate chips. Divide the batter between the pans and bake 18-20 minutes. Do not over bake. Let cool completely.

Frost with chocolate or white chocolate buttercream or alternate both with two pastry bags.

        Makes 24 brownies

* White Chocolate Buttercream and Chocolate Buttercream recipes are on the following page.

CHOCOLATE BUTTERCREAM:

1½ cups butter, soft
2 teaspoons milk
9 oz semisweet chocolate, melted, slightly cooled
1 teaspoon vanilla extract
2¼ cups icing sugar, sifted

In bowl of electric mixer, beat the butter for 3 minutes. Add the milk and beat until creamy. Add the melted chocolate, beat 2 minutes. Add the vanilla, beat 2 minutes. Add the icing sugar on low and beat until light and fluffy.

WHITE CHOCOLATE BUTTERCREAM:

1½ cups butter, soft
6 tablespoons milk
9 oz white chocolate, melted, slightly cooled
1 teaspoon vanilla extract
3 cups icing sugar, sifted

In bowl of electric mixer, beat the butter for 3 minutes. Add the milk and beat until creamy. Add the melted chocolate, beat 2 minutes. Add the vanilla, beat 2 minutes. Add the icing sugar on low and beat until light and fluffy.

Melting Chocolate: Place the chocolate in double boiler over simmering water, on low heat, for 5-10 minutes. Stir until melted. Remove pan from heat. Stir until smooth.

CAKE SQUARES

Basically, these are all of our single layer cakes that we cut into squares and serve on plates garnished with icing sugar, cocoa, drizzles of coulis or whipped cream studded with berries. They are less pretentious than the heavily frosted, layered, round cakes but every bit as delicious.

CHOCOLATE BANANA CAKE:

Hands down, our most popular cake!
    3 cups all purpose flour
    1½ teaspoon baking soda
    1½ teaspoon baking powder
    1 cup butter, soft
    2 eggs
    1 cup buttermilk
    4 bananas, mashed
    1 teaspoon vanilla extract
    1½ cups brown sugar
    1 tablespoon ground cinnamon
    1½ cups chocolate chips
Preheat oven to 350° F.

    Sift together flour, baking soda and baking powder. In bowl of electric mixer, cream butter and sugar. Add eggs, one at a time. Add dry ingredients alternating with the buttermilk. Incorporate the bananas and vanilla.

Combine brown sugar and cinnamon. Pour half the batter into a greased 13 x 9 inch baking pan. Sprinkle half the cinnamon sugar over the surface then half the chocolate chips. Pour remaining batter and spread evenly. Sprinkle remaining cinnamon sugar over surface then remaining chocolate chips.

Bake 1 hour 15 minutes rotating pan halfway through. Remove from oven and cool on wire rack.

Makes 12 squares

ORANGE WALNUT STREUSEL CAKE:

Add a cup of semisweet chocolate chips to the streusel if you like that orange-chocolate combination.

Cake:

   3 cups all purpose flour
   1½ teaspoons baking powder
   1½ teaspoons baking soda
   1⅓ cups sugar
   ¾ cup butter, soft
   3 eggs
   1 tablespoon grated orange zest
   1½ teaspoons vanilla extract
   1½ cups buttermilk
   ¼ cup orange juice

Streusel:

   1½ cups packed brown sugar
   1 tablespoon ground cinnamon
   6 tablespoons butter, cold
   1½ cups walnuts, chopped

Preheat oven to 350° F.

Cake:

Sift the flour, baking powder and baking soda together. In bowl of electric mixer cream the butter and sugar. Add the eggs, one at a time, then the zest and vanilla. Incorporate the dry ingredients and the buttermilk alternately. Add the orange juice. Beat until smooth.

Filling:

For the streusel, combine brown sugar and cinnamon. Cut in the butter. Mix in the nuts.

Pour half the cake batter into a greased 13 x 9 inch baking pan. Scatter half the streusel over the batter. Top with remaining batter and streusel. Bake for 1 hour 15 minutes, rotating pan and tenting with aluminum foil halfway through baking time. Cool on wire rack.

    Makes 12 squares

LEMON BLUEBERRY CAKE:

Moist and light and the taste is just right.

Cake:

1 cup butter, soft
2 cups sugar
4 eggs
3 cups all purpose flour
½ teaspoon baking soda
½ teaspoon salt
1 cup buttermilk
2½ tablespoons lemon zest, finely grated
2½ tablespoons fresh lemon juice
1 cup fresh blueberries (or frozen)

Glaze:

½ cup icing sugar
½ cup lemon juice
3 tablespoons lemon zest, finely grated

Preheat oven to 325° F.

Cake:

In bowl of electric mixer beat the butter and sugar until creamy. Add the eggs, one at a time. Sift the flour, baking soda and salt together and add to the creamed mixture alternating with the buttermilk. Stir in the lemon zest and juice. Fold in the blueberries.

Pour into a greased 13 x 9 inch baking pan and bake 1 hour 15 minutes. When cake is slightly cooled, prick the surface with a toothpick and drizzle the glaze over the cake. Throw a few more blueberries over the surface, if desired.

Glaze:

Mix all ingredients. Whisk well before using.

Makes 12 squares

PRALINE CAKE:

This cake is naughty and nice with its wholesome oatmeal base and decadent caramelized topping.

Cake:

   1¼ cups boiling water
   1 cup rolled oats, old fashioned
   2 cups all purpose flour
   2 teaspoons baking powder
   ¾ teaspoon cinnamon
   ½ teaspoon baking soda
   ½ teaspoon salt
   ¼ teaspoon nutmeg
   ¾ cup butter
   1 cup sugar
   ½ cup brown sugar
   1 teaspoon vanilla extract
   2 eggs

Topping:

   ¼ cup butter
   2 tablespoons cream
   ½ cup brown sugar
   ¾ cup pecans, chopped
   $1/3$ cup coconut, sweetened, shredded

Preheat oven to 350° F.

Cake:

In bowl, combine boiling water with oats. Let stand for 20 minutes. Sift together flour, baking powder, cinnamon, baking soda, salt and nutmeg.

In bowl of electric mixer, cream butter one minute. Add the sugars and cream 30 seconds. Add vanilla and eggs. Add dry ingredients alternating with oatmeal mixture. Pour into a greased 13 x 9 inch baking pan. Bake 40 minutes.

Topping:

In meantime, melt butter and cream in saucepan. Add brown sugar and heat until sugar dissolves. Fold in pecans and coconut. Spread topping over slightly cooled cake and place pans under a broiler until caramelized (a few minutes– watching like a hawk, so it doesn't burn).
        Makes 24 squares

CHOCOLATE COCA COLA CAKE:

This sounds like it will be popular with kids but it's the adults who keep coming back—especially the men—for some strange reason.

Cake:

2 cups self rising flour
2 cups sugar
1 cup butter
3 tablespoons cocoa
1 cup coca cola
1½ cups miniature marshmallows
2 eggs, beaten
1 teaspoon baking soda
2 teaspoons vanilla extract
½ cup buttermilk

Preheat oven to 350° F.

In bowl, combine flour and sugar.
In saucepan, put cocoa, cola, butter, marshmallows and bring to a boil. Combine with the flour-sugar mixture and mix well.

In separate bowl, combine eggs, buttermilk, baking soda and vanilla. Beat this into the first mixture. Pour batter into a greased and floured 13 x 9 inch baking pan. Bake 35 minutes or until cake tests done. Remove from oven. Ice cake while still warm.

Icing:

½ cup butter
1 tablespoon cocoa
6 tablespoons coca cola
2 cups icing sugar
½ cup pecans, chopped

In saucepan, bring butter, cocoa and coca cola to a boil. Stir in the icing sugar until smooth. Fold in the pecans. Frost warm cake with warm icing.

Makes 12 squares

Pies

It's been said that the hand that cuts the pie rules the world. That's how well loved pie is around the globe. All of the following recipes will let you rule your world, or at least rock it.

PECAN BOURBON PIE:

Every day can be thanksgiving because everyone will thank you for baking this gorgeous pie.
    9 inch unbaked pie shell
    3 large eggs
    ½ cup dark brown sugar
    ½ cup light brown sugar
    ²/₃ cup light corn syrup
    ¼ cup bourbon
    1 teaspoon coarse salt
    2 cups pecan halves
Preheat oven to 350° F.

    In bowl of electric mixer, beat the eggs then whisk in the dark and light brown sugars. Add the corn syrup, butter, bourbon, salt and beat until combined. Pour the filling into the pie shell and scatter the pecan halves over the surface.

    Bake 55 minutes until the filling is puffed and just set in the center.
        Makes 8 servings

DOUBLE KEY LIME PIE:

"Double" because it has two layers making it twice as good as any other key lime pie.

Crust:

¾ cup granola
¾ cup graham cracker crumbs
¼ cup butter, melted
3 tablespoons sugar

Preheat oven to 325° F.

Blend granola in food processor until coarsely ground. Transfer to bowl. Add cracker crumbs, sugar and melted butter and mix well. Press into bottom and upsides of 9 inch deep dish glass pie dish. Bake 8 minutes. Cool completely.

Baked Filling:

½ cup lime juice
4 egg yolks
14 oz can sweetened condensed milk

Whisk together lime juice, egg yolks and condensed milk. Pour into pie crust and bake 25 minutes or until set. Cool to room temperature.

Chilled Filling:

8 oz package cream cheese, soft
½ cup sweetened condensed milk
¼ cup lime juice
2 tablespoons sugar
1 teaspoon vanilla extract

In bowl of electric mixer, beat cream cheese, condensed milk, lime juice, sugar and vanilla until smooth. Spread evenly over cooled, baked filling. Cover and chill at least 4 hours or overnight.

Decorate with dollops of sweetened whipped cream and lime peel shavings.
Makes 8 servings

MILE HIGH APPLE PIE:

Mounds of crisp makes this pie vertical but it can be replaced with a top-crust and will still be the best apple pie you've ever made.
- 9 inch unbaked pie shell
- 4½ lbs Golden Delicious Apples
- 1 tablespoon fresh lemon juice
- 8 tablespoons butter
- 1 cup packed brown sugar
- ¼ teaspoon cinnamon
- 1½ tablespoons flour

Preheat oven to 350° F.

Peel, halve and core the apples. Cut into wedges and toss with the lemon juice in a large bowl. Melt the butter in a 12 "skillet over low heat; stir in brown sugar. Add the apples, stir to coat then increase heat to med-high. Cook the apples, stirring occasionally until tender but not mushy, about 15 minutes.

Transfer apples to a baking sheet with their juices. Sprinkle the flour and cinnamon over the apples and stir to combine. Let apples cool down to room temperature, about 40 minutes.

Spoon apples with their juices into pie shell. Cover the apples with half the crisp. Bake 25 minutes. Cover the pie with the remaining crisp and return to the oven for another 25 minutes.

Makes 8 servings

Crisp:

- 1 cup all purpose flour
- 1 cup rolled oats
- ½ cup brown sugar
- ¼ cup sugar
- a pinch of salt
- ½ teaspoon cinnamon
- 8 tablespoons butter

Combine flour, oats, sugars, salt and cinnamon. Rub in the butter until it is crumbly. Fold in nuts, if desired.

RHUBARD ALMOND TART:

European-style, elegant tart.

Filling:

¾ cup sugar
¾ cup icing sugar
12 tablespoons butter
2 cups rhubarb, chopped,
2 eggs
¾ cup ground almonds
$1/3$ cup all purpose flour
3 tablespoons milk
$1/3$ cup good quality raspberry jam

Pastry:

$1^2/_3$ cups all purpose flour
½ cup icing sugar
8 tablespoons butter, cold
1 egg

Make pastry first. Put flour and icing sugar in food processor. Add butter and pulse until it resembles coarse crumbs. Add egg. Pulse until dough forms into a ball. Wrap dough in plastic wrap and chill 1 hour.
Preheat oven to 350° F.

Grease a 9 inch, loose bottom, tart pan. Roll dough and line the tart pan with pastry. Refrigerate 15 minutes. Put a sheet of parchment paper over surface of pastry and weigh down with uncooked rice. Bake 10 minutes and remove the paper and rice. Continue to bake another 5 minutes. For filling, in saucepan, combine the ¾ cup sugar with 1¾ cups water. Heat over low until sugar dissolves. Add rhubarb and simmer 3 minutes, drain but reserve the liquid. Reduce the liquid over medium until syrupy. Set aside. In bowl, beat butter and icing sugar until fluffy. Beat in eggs, one at a time. Fold in almonds and flour. Stir in milk.
Spread jam over bottom of pie shell. Add half the rhubarb and spread.
Makes 8-10 servings

FRUIT AND CREAM TART:

This is one visually stunning pie but much more impressive than difficult.

>Pastry dough to fit 12 inch pizza pan
>3 oz cream cheese
>¾ cup sugar
>1 tablespoon milk
>1 tablespoon grated orange rind
>⅔ cup heavy cream
>2 tablespoons corn starch
>¼ cup water
>½ cup orange juice
>¼ cup lemon juice
>1 pint strawberries, sliced
>2 bananas, sliced
>12 oz can mandarin orange segments, drained

Preheat oven to 375° F.

Reserve 2 or 3 pretty strawberries. Roll pastry to fit the pizza pan. Crimp edges and prick surface with a fork. Bake 10 minutes.

Combine cream cheese, ¼ cup of the sugar, milk and orange rind in a bowl. Beat with electric mixer until smooth. Gradually add heavy cream, beating until thick and creamy. Spread over cool crust and chill in refrigerator.

Combine remaining ½ cup sugar and corn starch in saucepan. Stir in water, orange juice, lemon juice and cook over medium, stirring constantly, until mixture boils. Cook 1 minute more. Remove from heat and let cool.

Start at the crimped edge of crust and form a circle of sliced strawberries, next a circle of sliced bananas, next mandarin segments, working towards the center of the pie. Spoon cooled sauce evenly over fruit. Chill in fridge at least 2 hours. Decorate gap in middle of pie with reserved strawberries.

Makes 12-16 servings

COCONUT CREAM PIE:

Billowy, fluffy, dreamy!
- 9 inch baked pie shell
- 3 tablespoons flour
- ½ cup sugar
- 1 large egg yolk
- 2 large eggs
- 1 teaspoon vanilla extract
- ½ teaspoon coconut extract
- 1½ cups whole milk
- 1½ cups coconut, sweetened

In bowl, whisk flour, sugar, egg yolk and eggs.

In saucepan, over medium heat, bring milk and coconut to a simmer. Add egg mixture, slowly, to hot milk mixture, whisking constantly for 3 to 4 minutes. Remove from heat and stir in the vanilla and coconut extracts. Transfer to bowl and press plastic wrap directly on surface of custard. Chill at least 2 hours. Pour filling in crust. Cover and chill overnight. Prepare topping.

Topping:

- 1½ cups chilled heavy cream
- 3 tablespoons sugar
- ½ teaspoon coconut extract
- ½ cup toasted coconut

In bowl of electric mixer, beat heavy cream, sugar and coconut extract until stiff peaks form. Spread over top of pie and sprinkle the toasted coconut over surface to decorate.

Makes 8 servings

RAISIN BUTTER TARTS:
The syrup will dribble down your chin and you won't even care.
24 unbaked pie tart shells
2 cups brown sugar
2 cups corn syrup
½ lb butter (no substitutes)
8 eggs
1 teaspoon salt
2 teaspoons vanilla extract
2 teaspoons white vinegar
2 cups sultana raisins (or other dark raisins)
Preheat oven to 350° F.

In saucepan, bring brown sugar and corn syrup to a boil. Boil for 5 minutes. Add butter to mixture and stir until melted.

In large bowl, whisk eggs slightly and gradually add the hot mixture, beating constantly. Add salt, vanilla and vinegar. Mix well.

Place 1 heaping tablespoon of raisins into each tart shell and pour in hot mixture up to the rim.

Bake for 20 minutes or until pastry is golden. Cool before removing from tins.
Makes 24 tarts

Pies

PERFECT PASTRY DOUGH:

Well worth the effort for this homemade, flaky pie crust–perfect every time.
    2½ cups all purpose flour
    1 teaspoon salt
    3 teaspoons sugar
    ½ cup butter, cold, unsalted
    ½ cup shortening, cold
    ice water

In food processor, pulse flour, salt and sugar. Add butter and shortening; pulse until mixture resembles coarse crumbs. Add $1/3$ cup ice water and pulse until moistened. Squeeze a little dough between your fingers; it should come together. If it crumbles, add 1 tablespoon of ice water and pulse.

Gather the dough into a ball on a lightly floured work surface. Divide in half. Cover with plastic wrap and refrigerate for a minimum of 30 minutes.

Return dough to lightly floured surface and roll one ball into a 13 inch round. Fit into a 9 inch pie plate and trim the overhang to ½ inch. Crimp edges if using only the bottom crust.

For top crust, roll the second dough ball into a 12 inch round. Moisten the pie rim with wet pastry brush. Center the top crust over the filling in the pie shell and press the rim to seal. With scissors or sharp knife, trim the top crust to a ½ inch overhang, fold under and crimp edges. Pierce holes in top of pie with fork or knife.

    Makes a 9 inch double crust pie

Desserts

We have many popular desserts that don't fit in the category of pies, cakes, bars, etc. so I have given them their own well-deserved chapter.

RICE PUDDING:

Everyone–and I mean "everyone"–asks for this recipe.
    1 tablespoon vanilla extract
    6 cups whole milk
    ¾ cup sugar
    ¾ cup arborio rice
    ¼ teaspoon salt

In saucepan, put milk, vanilla and sugar and heat to boiling over medium, stirring occasionally. Stir in rice and bring back to a boil. Reduce heat to low, cover and simmer for 1¼ hours or until very creamy and thickened, stirring occasionally.

Remove pan from heat. Stir in salt. Transfer to a large bowl and cool slightly. Cover and refrigerate at least 6 hours.

Serve with sprinkling of cinnamon and pure maple syrup, if desired.

RUM RAISIN RICE PUDDING:

Prepare as above, but start by combining in a bowl:
  ¾ cup raisins
  2 tablespoons dark rum

Set aside and add to the rice at the same time you add the salt (at the end of the cooling time).

BREAD PUDDING WITH BOURBON SAUCE:

Something of an american classic–at least the bourbon part.

Pudding:

    5 eggs
    ¾ cup sugar
    2 teaspoons vanilla extract
    1-2 teaspoons ground cinnamon, to taste
    ⅛ teaspoon nutmeg
    ½ teaspoon salt
    3 cups heavy cream
    4½ cup sourdough bread, torn into 1 inch pieces
    ⅓ cup pecans, chopped
Preheat oven to 350° F.

    In bowl, whisk eggs, sugar, vanilla, cinnamon, nutmeg and salt . Stir in the cream until well blended. Add the bread, tossing to fully saturate. Set aside for 15 minutes.

    Divide bread mixture among eight greased custard cups or ramekins. Sprinkle the nuts over the tops. Put ramekins in a baking pan and add enough water to come half way up the sides of the cups. Bake 50 minutes or until knife inserted in center comes out almost clean. Serve the warm bourbon sauce on the side.
        Makes 8 servings

Bourbon Sauce:

    ½ cup sugar
    ½ cup butter
    ½ cup heavy cream
    ¼ cup bourbon

    In saucepan, combine sugar, butter and heavy cream and stir constantly over low heat until mixture reaches a low, rolling boil. Remove from heat. Stir in the bourbon.

CRÈME BRULÉE:

Serve with a lace cookie or rolled wafer for dipping.
    5 egg yolks
    ½ cup sugar
    3 cups heavy cream
    1 vanilla bean
    1 tablespoon orange liqueur—such as Grand Marnier
    raw sugar
Preheat oven to 325° F.

    In bowl of electric mixer, beat egg yolks and sugar on low until combined. In meantime, scald the cream in a small saucepan until steaming hot but not boiling. On low speed, slowly add cream to eggs. Split the vanilla bean down the middle, scrape out the seeds and add to the egg-cream mixture. Add the orange liqueur and stir just until combined. Pour this mixture into six 8 oz ramekins until almost full. Place ramekins in a baking pan and add enough hot water to come halfway up sides of ramekins.

    Bake 35 to 40 minutes or until they appear set when shaken slightly. Remove ramekins from the water and cool to room temperature. Refrigerate until firm.

    Before serving, sprinkle tops of custards with raw sugar and place under the broiler or heat with a kitchen torch until sugar caramelizes.
        Makes 6 servings

Desserts 91

NO BAKE CHEESECAKE CUPS:

Use clear, plastic beverage cups or plastic wine cups. Just grab them out of the freezer a few hours before serving.

- 3 tablespoons sugar
- 1½ cups vanilla cookie crumbs, finely ground
- 4 tablespoons butter, melted
- 2 packages cream cheese, room temperature
- 1 cup sugar
- 3 tablespoons fresh lime juice
- ½ cup heavy cream
- 14 oz can cherry or blueberry pie filling

Stir together the cookie crumbs and the 3 tablespoons of sugar. Add the melted butter and combine well. Divide this mixture among the cups.

In bowl, with electric mixer, beat the cream cheese for 3 minutes. Add the sugar in a steady stream until well incorporated. Add the lime juice, beat until creamy.

In separate bowl, beat the heavy cream until stiff peaks form. Gently fold this mixture into the cream cheese mixture. Divide this between the cups with the cookie crumb mixture. Freeze the cups for 1 hour. Refrigerate until ready to serve. Top with the fruit filling. Garnish with sweetened whipped cream, if desired.

Makes 10-12 servings

MOJITO GRANITA:

Granitas are so refreshing that they are popular all year long—even the blizzard months.

    1 cup sugar
    3 cups water
    1 bunch mint leaves, reserving for garnish
    ½ cup lime juice
    ½ cup white rum

Place sugar and water in a saucepan and heat over med-high until mixture comes to a boil and sugar is dissolved. Remove from heat and let cool. Put the syrup in a blender with the remaining ingredients. Blend 1 minute. Pour into a 9 x 13 inch metal pan. Place in freezer. Scrape with a fork every hour to break up the ice crystals. Repeat between 4 and 6 hours or until of desired consistency.

    Garnish with reserved mint leaves.
           Makes 8 servings

FRUIT AND YOGURT PARFAIT:

For anyone who won't give up "delicious" in exchange for "healthy."
    2 cups vanilla yogurt
    1 cup fieldberries, fresh or frozen
    4 tablespoons maple syrup
    1 cup granola

Use 4 parfait glasses. In one glass, place a heaping tablespoon of fieldberries, ¼ cup vanilla yogurt, 1 tablespoon maple syrup, another ¼ cup vanilla yogurt, another heaping tablespoon fieldberries and ¼ cup granola. Layer the remaining 3 parfait glasses in this order.

        Makes 4 large parfait glasses

Desserts 95

Cinnamon bun

Author and Granddaughter share a latte

Fruit and yogurt parfait

Desserts 97

Layered Latte

Double Key lime pie

Whiskey Tispy Fudge Cake

Espresso Martinis

Cakes

You can't run a good coffee shop with good signature cakes–really good! And these are good cakes–really good!

TIRAMISU:

The light, dreamy, Italian Bistro cake that's loved around the world.
  1 lb marscapone
  ¼ cup sugar
  2 tablespoons amaretto or other almond liqueur
  1 cup heavy cream
  24 Italian Lady Fingers
  1 cup brewed strong coffee, room temperature
  1 cup chopped semisweet chocolate
  cocoa
Preheat oven to 350° F.

In bowl, whip the marscapone, sugar and Amaretto. In separate bowl, whip the heavy cream until stiff peaks form. Fold the cream into the marscapone mixture.

Lightly dip the lady fingers into the coffee. Arrange the lady fingers in bottom of an 8 inch springform pan. Spread half the masrcapone mixture over the lady fingers. Sprinkle with half the semi sweet chocolate. Repeat this operation with another layer of lady fingers, another layer or masrcapone and the remaining chocolate. Cover with plastic wrap. Refrigerate overnight.

Unmold and sprinkle with cocoa.
Makes 10-12 servings

CINNAMON STREUSEL COFFEE CAKE:

Perfectly sweet–the perfect coffee break cake.
¾ cup butter, soft
1½ cups sugar
3 eggs
2 teaspoons vanilla extract
1¼ cups sour cream
2½ cups cake flour
2 teaspoons baking powder
½ teaspoon baking soda
Preheat oven to 350° F.

In bowl of electric mixer, cream butter and sugar for 5 minutes. Add eggs one at a time, beating well after each addition. Beat in vanilla and sour cream.

In separate bowl, sift cake flour, baking powder, baking soda and salt. Add dry ingredients to batter on low speed, just until combined. Spread half the batter in greased and floured 10 inch tube pan. Sprinkle with half the streusel. Pour remaining batter on top and sprinkle with remaining streusel. Bake 1 hour.

When cool, invert onto serving platter. Drizzle cake with store bought caramel sauce or dust with icing sugar.

Makes 10-12 servings

Streusel:
¼ cup brown sugar
½ cup all purpose flour
1½ teaspoons cinnamon
½ teaspoon salt
3 tablespoons butter, cold
¾ cup nuts, chopped (opt)

In bowl, mix brown sugar, flour, cinnamon and salt. Work in butter with fingers. Add nuts.

WHISKEY TIPSY FUDGE CAKE:

I can't begin to tell you how good this cake is but these three words should suffice–whiskey–fudge–cake!

6 oz bittersweet chocolate, melted, cooled a little
¼ cup instant coffee crystals
¼ cups boiling water
1¼ cups cold water
½ cup whiskey
1 cup butter, soft
2 cups sugar
1 teaspoon vanilla extract
3 eggs
2 cups flour
1 teaspoon baking soda
¼ teaspoon salt
½ cup pecans, halved

Preheat oven to 325° F.

Grease and flour a Bundt pan then scatter the pecans in bottom of pan.
In bowl, sift flour, baking soda and salt together. Set aside. Dissolve the coffee crystals in the boiling water then stir in the cold water and whiskey. Set aside.

In bowl of electric mixer, cream the butter and sugar until light and fluffy. Beat in the vanilla and the eggs, one at a time, beating well after each addition. With the mixer on low, pour in the chocolate and mix well. Add the flour and coffee-whiskey mixture to the butter mixture alternately and mix until well combined.

Pour into prepared pan and bake for 1 hour to 1¼ hours or until cake tests done. Cool cake 10 minutes on rack. Prick bottom of cake with a toothpick. Spoon one half cup of the whiskey glaze over bottom of cake. Cool 15 minutes. Invert cake on plate. Pour one half cup glaze over top of cake. Sprinkle cake with icing sugar if desired.

Makes 12 servings

Whiskey Glaze:

½ cup butter

¼ cup water
1 cup sugar
½ cup whiskey

Melt butter in saucepan. Stir in water and sugar. Boil, stirring constantly, for 5 minutes. Remove from heat. Stir in whiskey.

CHOCOLATE AMARETTO CAKE:

So dark, so smooth, so rich–and it's from a mix.
   18.25 oz package Devils Food Cake Mix
   1 1/3 cups water
   3 eggs
   ½ cup oil
   ¾ cup Amaretto or other almond liqueur
   ¾ teaspoon almond extract
   3 cups dark chocolate chips
   ¼ cup butter
   ¼ cup heavy cream
   1 cup icing sugar
   2/3 cup sour cream
   1 cup slivered almonds, toasted
Preheat oven to 350° F.

In bowl of electric mixer, beat cake mix, water, eggs, oil, 3 tablespoons Amaretto and ½ teaspoon almond extract until smooth. Fold in 1 cup chocolate chips. Divide batter among three 9 inch round cake pans which have been greased and floured.

Bake 15 minutes or until cakes test done. When cool, brush each cake layer with 2 tablespoons Amaretto. Ice with Chocolate–Sour Cream frosting and press almonds around bottom 2 inches of cake. Refrigerate at least 2 hours.

To make frosting, in saucepan combine cream and butter. Bring to a simmer over med-low heat until butter melts. Remove from heat and add remaining 2 cups chocolate chips, whisking to melt. Add remaining 3 tablespoons Amaretto. Cool 5 minutes. Beat in sour cream, remaining ¼ teaspoon almond extract then the icing sugar. Beat until smooth and creamy. Refrigerate until of spreading consistency or about 10 minutes.

      Makes 12 servings

MANGO TANGO CARROT CAKE:
Mango, carrots, pineapple, coconut–this cake has it all.

3 eggs
1 cup oil
1 cup brown sugar
1½ cups cake flour
1 teaspoon baking soda
2 teaspoons ground cinnamon
1 cup grated carrots
¾ cup nuts, chopped
14 oz can pineapple, crushed, drained
1 mango, peeled, thinly sliced
¼ cup sweetened, shaved coconut

Preheat oven to 350° F.

In bowl of electric mixer, beat eggs, oil and brown sugar until light. In separate bowl, sift flour, baking soda and cinnamon. Add to creamed mixture, on low speed, until just combined. Fold in nuts, carrots and pineapple. Pour into a 9 inch springform pan which has been greased and lined with parchment. Bake for 1 hour or until it tests done. Cool cake before removing mold. Split cake into two layers. Spread half the icing over bottom layer. Top with the mango slices. Replace top layer of cake and spread with remaining icing. Sprinkle with shaved coconut.

    Makes 8-10 servings

Cream Cheese Icing:

½ cup butter, soft
1 cup cream cheese, soft
1 teaspoon vanilla extract
2 cups icing sugar, sifted
1 tablespoon lemon juice

With mixer, beat butter, cream cheese and vanilla until smooth. Beat in icing sugar and lemon juice until light and creamy.

SKYSCRAPER CHOCOLATE CARAMEL CAKE:

A 6 layer cake, hence "skyscraper", combining vanilla, chocolate and caramel.

    1 cup butter, soft
    2 cups sugar
    4 eggs
    3 cups self rising flour
    1 cup milk
    1 teaspoon vanilla extract
Preheat oven to 350° F.

In bowl of electric mixer, cream butter until light and fluffy. Add sugar gradually and beat 6 minutes. Add eggs, one at a time. Add flour alternately with the milk. Add the vanilla. Pour batter into 3 greased and floured 9 inch round cake pans. Bake 15-20 minutes. Cool in pans 10 minutes. Cool completely on wire racks. Split each cake into 2 layers. Frost between the layers alternating the chocolate and caramel frosting. Frost top of cake with the chocolate frosting and drizzle the sides with caramel. Garnish with chocolate shavings.

Makes 12 servings

Chocolate Frosting:

    1 cup sugar
    $1/3$ cup cocoa
    ½ cup butter
    $2/3$ cup cream
    2 tablespoons corn syrup
    pinch of salt
    3 cups icing sugar, sifted
    1 teaspoon vanilla extract

In saucepan, put sugar to salt. Bring to a boil, simmer, stirring for 3 minutes. Remove from heat. Transfer to bowl. Beat in icing sugar and vanilla with mixer until fluffy. Thin with more cream if too thick.

Caramel Frosting:

    ½ cup butter
    1 cup packed dark brown sugar
    $1/3$ cup heavy cream

1 tablespoon vanilla extract
2 cups icing sugar, sifted

Melt butter in saucepan. Add brown sugar and heavy cream, cook over med-low until sugar is dissolved, about 2 minutes. Remove from heat. Transfer to a bowl. Beat in icing sugar and vanilla with mixer until fluffy. Thin with more cream if too thick.

COCO BANGO COCONUT CAKE:

The "Bango" comes from the rum. I have added fresh pineapple between the layers and transformed this into a "Pina Colada" cake.

Cake:

18.5 oz package golden cake mix
3 eggs
½ cup butter, soft
⅓ cup sweetened cream of coconut (not coconut milk)
⅓ cup water

Frosting:

2 x 8 oz packages cream cheese, soft
½ cup butter, soft
½ cup sweetened cream of coconut (not coconut milk)
¾ cup icing sugar
1 teaspoon vanilla extract
3 cups sweetened flaked coconut

Preheat oven to 375° F.

For Cake:

Combine cake mix, eggs, butter, cream of coconut and water in bowl of electric mixer. Beat on low, increase speed to medium and beat 4 minutes. Divide between two greased and buttered 9 inch cake pans. Bake 25 minutes. Cool in pans 10 minutes. Cool completely on wire racks.

For Frosting:

In bowl of electric mixer, beat cream cheese, butter, cream of coconut and vanilla until smooth. Gradually add icing sugar, beating until light and fluffy.

Assembling Cake:

Spread one cake layer with ¾ cup frosting. Sprinkle with ¾ cup flaked coconut. Top with second cake layer. Spread frosting on side and top of cake and press the remaining coconut over the entire surface of the cake (top and sides). Chill at least 1 hour.

Makes 12 servings

CREAMY CHEESECAKE:

Top with fresh berries, caramel, fruit topping, anything or nothing at all. This cheesecake, with its perfectly creamy texture, will be the star attraction.

Crust:

    1½ cups graham cracker crumbs
    2 tablespoons sugar
    5 tablespoons butter, melted

Filling:

    1 lb cream cheese, soft
    1 cup sugar
    6 egg yolks
    3 tablespoons fresh lemon juice
    1½ teaspoons vanilla extract
    ¼ teaspoon salt
    3 cups sour cream

Prehean oven to 350° F.

Blend all crust ingredients and press in bottom and partway up sides of a greased 8 inch springform pan. Wrap the outside of the pan with a double layer of aluminum foil.

In the bowl of an electric mixer, beat the cream cheese and sugar for 3 minutes—or until very smooth. Beat in egg yolks. Add lemon juice, vanilla and salt, beating until blended. Fold in the sour cream.

Pour batter in prepared pan. Set in a baking pan and pour in hot water to 1 inch depth. Bake for 45 minutes. Without opening the door, turn off the oven and let the cake cool for 1 hour. Transfer cake to wire rack and cool to room temperature, about 1 hour. Cover with plastic wrap and refrigerate overnight.

        Makes 12 servings

BREAKFAST

Like most "Coffee Shops" we don't have a large kitchen area. In fact, for our breakfast menu we rely on a small pancake griddle and our toaster grill. You can use your toaster, frying pan or oven to create the same easy, bistro style dishes.

BAGEL WITH RICOTTA:

Ricotta is lighter and more delicate than cream cheese.
- 1 sesame bagel, split
- ¼ cup ricotta cheese
- 1 tablespoon olive oil
- 1 basil leaf

Toast the bagel then spread with the ricotta. Place on serving plate then drizzle the olive oil over the bagel. Garnish with a basil leaf.

Makes 1 serving

MOKA BUTTER:

Serve with bagels, muffins, french toast, croissants or scones
- 1/2 cup butter, soft
- ¼ cup toasted pecans, chopped
- 2 tablespoons chocolate syrup
- 1 tablespoon prepared coffee, cooled

Beat all ingredients together. Let rest at room temperature for one hour.

BACON AND EGG BAGUETTE:

An easy, upscale egg breakfast sandwich.
- Small french baguette, split in two
- 2 eggs, beaten
- 1 tablespoon milk
- 2 slices bacon, cooked
- ¼ cup Swiss cheese, shredded
- Salt/Freshly ground black pepper
- Preheat broiler

Combine the eggs and milk with a fork and scramble up the eggs in a small non stick frying pan until just cooked through.

Lay the baguette, cut side up, on a small baking pan. Put the scrambled eggs on one side of the bread and the bacon on the other side. Cover both sides with the cheese and pass under the broiler until melted. Season with salt and pepper.

Makes 1 serving

HAM AND BRIE CROISSANT:

Serve on a plate with sliced tomatoes on a bed of greens.
- 1 croissant, split lengthwise
- Dijon mustard, to taste
- 3 slices black forest ham
- Brie cheese, two slices
- Salt/Freshly ground black pepper

Preheat broiler

Place croissant, cut side up on a baking pan. Spread Dijon on both sides of croissant. Layer both sides with the sliced ham and top with the brie. Pass under a broiler until the cheese melts. Serve with salt and freshly ground pepper on the side.

Makes 1 serving

NUTELLA BANANA CRÊPES:

Crêpes with chocolate peanut butter and bananas! What's wrong with that?

Crêpes:

1 cup + 2 tablespoons milk
2 large eggs
1 cup all purpose flour
2 tablespoons sugar
3 tablespoons butter, melted, cooled
¼ teaspoons salt

Blend milk, eggs, flour, sugar, 2 tablespoons butter and salt in blender, until batter is smooth, about 1 minute. Let batter stand at room temperature 1 hour (prevents tough crêpes). Heat 1 teaspoon butter over medium heat in a 10 inch non stick skillet. Pour ¼ cup batter in skillet, tilting to coat bottom evenly. Cook about 1½ minutes each side, or until golden. Make 7 more crêpes in the same manner.

Filling:

8 tablespoons Nutella
4 bananas, sliced

Spread entire surface of crêpe with 1 tablespoon nutella. Layer ½ sliced banana and roll up jelly roll style. Dust with icing sugar.
   Makes 8 crêpes

APRICOT BRANDY CRÊPES:

$2/3$ cup apricot jam
1 tablespoon brandy

In small bowl, mix the jam and the brandy. Prepare crêpes as above. Spread crêpes all over with jam. Roll up jelly roll style. Dust with icing sugar.

        Makes 8 crêpes

Note: crêpes without filling can be made 24 hours ahead and kept chilled, in airtight containers. Reheat in 350° F oven 1 minute.

MORNING GLORY HAM AND EGGS:

The eggs are baked in the slices of ham and resemble beautiful flowers.
    ¼ cup mushrooms, finely chopped
    ¼ cup red onion, finely chopped
    2 tablespoons butter
    2 tablespoons cream
    1 tablespoon tarragon, finely chopped
    12 slices black forest ham
    12 eggs, large
    Salt/Freshly ground black pepper
Preheat oven to 400° F.

In small frying pan, over medium heat, cook mushrooms and onions in butter until tender and liquid is evaporated, about 10 minutes. Remove from heat and stir in cream, tarragon, salt and pepper.

Fit 1 slice of ham into each of 12 lightly oiled muffin cups. Divide mushroom mixture among cups and crack 1 egg in each. Bake about 15 minutes or until whites are cooked but yolks are still runny. Season with salt and pepper. Remove from tins carefully.
        12 cups, or 6 servings

116   Have a Java

Quiche

A slice of quiche with a side of salad makes a terrific brunch, lunch or light supper. They are also greatly appreciated by our vegetarian clientele so the last two recipes are for our favorite meatless quiches. For the pie shell, you can use the recipe given on page 86 for "Perfect pastry dough" or go with store bought shells. I have also included two quiche dough recipes in this chapter.

BACON AND LEEK QUICHE:

Use extra filling to make an awesome omelet.
    9 inch unbaked pie shell
    4 leeks, chopped
    2 tablespoons butter
    3 eggs, large
    1 tablespoon mustard
    1½ cups cream, heavy or 15%–warm
    6 strips bacon
    1½ cups mozzarella cheese, shredded
    1 tablespoon parsley, chopped
    Salt/Freshly ground black pepper
Preheat oven to 350° F.

    Sauté leeks in butter for 5 minutes. Season with salt and pepper and put in pie shell. Blend eggs, mustard, warm cream in blender for 30 seconds. Pour over the leeks and scatter the bacon on top. Cover with the cheese and sprinkle with parsley.

Bake in oven for 40 minutes or until center is set.
Makes 8 servings

KILLER CRAB QUICHE:

The crab isn't the killer—the quiche is!
    9 inch unbaked pie shell
    ½ lb lump crab meat, picked over
    4 eggs
    2 cups heavy cream
    3 tablespoons chives, finely chopped
    3 tablespoons parsley, finely chopped
    ½ teaspoon seafood seasoning
    Pinch of nutmeg
    1 cup Swiss cheese, shredded
    Salt/Freshly ground black pepper
Preheat oven to 350° F.

Cut crab meat into ½ inch pieces. In bowl, whisk eggs, cream, herbs, seafood seasoning, salt and pepper. Stir in cheese and crabmeat. Pour into unbaked pie shell and bake 40 to 50 minutes or until filling is puffy and center is set.
      Makes 8 servings

SPINACH, MUSHROOM AND BACON QUICHE:

Rivals pizza!
- 9 inch unbaked pie shell
- 2 cups mushrooms, sliced
- 2 tablespoons butter
- 6 strips bacon, cooked, crumbled
- 10 oz package frozen spinach, thawed, excess liquid squeezed out
- 1½ cups Swiss cheese, shredded
- 6 eggs
- 1½ cups heavy cream
- Salt/Freshly ground black pepper

Preheat oven to 375° F.

Sauté mushrooms in butter until soft, 5 minutes. Add spinach and cook 1 minute more. Put into bottom of pie shell. Cover mushrooms and spinach with the cheese. Blend eggs, cream, salt and pepper in blender for 30 seconds. Pour egg mixture over the cheese. Bake 35 to 45 minutes.

Makes 8 servings

THREE CHEESE ASPARAGUS QUICHE:

Cheese and asparagus anything is good.
- 1 unbaked 10 inch pie shell
- 1-2 teaspoons ground paprika
- 1 pound asparagus (1 bunch), trimmed, cooked
- 4 eggs, beaten
- 2/3 cup cream, warmed
- 2/3 cup fontina cheese, grated
- ½ cup cheddar cheese, shredded
- ½ cup blue cheese, crumbled
- 1/3 cup green onions, sliced
- Salt/Freshly ground black pepper
- ½ red pepper, julienned

Preheat oven to 350° F.

Sprinkle the paprika over the pie shell and then place the asparagus in the bottom.

In a large bowl, whisk the remaining ingredients except for the red pepper and pour this over the asparagus. Sprinkle the red pepper over the top. Bake for 35-40 minutes.

Makes 6–8 servings

HOT AND SPICY QUICHE DOUGH:

Sometimes we're in the mood to heat things up.
    $1^2/_3$ cup whole wheat flour
    ½ teaspoon crushed red pepper flakes
    ½ teaspoon kosher salt
    1 teaspoon dry mustard
    ¾ cup butter, cold
    $^2/_3$ cup swiss cheese, shredded very fine
    $^1/_3$ cup water

In a bowl, combine the first four ingredients. Cut in the butter with a pastry blender or two knives until mixture resembles coarse crumbs. Incorporate the cheese then add the water, all at once, and stir.

Form the dough into a ball, wrap in plastic and refrigerate 30 minutes. Separate the ball in two and roll each half to fit a 10 inch pie plate.
        Makes 2 pie shells

TEX-MEX QUICHE:

Serve this flavorful quiche with sour cream and salsa.
- 1 pound ground beef
- ½ teaspoon ground coriander
- ½ teaspoon ground cumin
- 1 teaspoon chili spice or cayenne
- 1 unbaked 10" pie shell
- 4 eggs, beaten
- 11/2 cups cheddar cheese, shredded
- ½ cup cream, warmed
- 2 green onions, sliced
- Salt/Freshly ground black pepper
- 1 avocado, peeled pitted and sliced
- 2 tortilla shells, 10 inch
- ½ cup salsa

Preheat oven to 375 ° F.

Fry the first four ingredients in a skillet until all the pink is gone from the ground beef. Drain any fat and season with salt and pepper. Place the beef mixture in the bottom of the pie shell.

In a bowl, whisk together the eggs, ½ cup of the cheese, the cream, green onions, salt and pepper. Pour half of this mixture over the ground beef. Top with a tortilla shell which has been trimmed to fit the inside of the pie shell. Lay the slices of avocado on the tortilla shell and pour the remaining egg mixture over this. Top with the second tortilla shell and spread the salsa over it. Sprinkle the remaining cheese over the top of the quiche. Bake in the oven for 40 minutes.

Makes 6-8 servings.

ITALIAN TOMATOES AND HEART OF PALM QUICHE:

So pretty—so delicious—so Bistro!
- 1 unbaked 10 inch pie shell
- 12 Italian tomatoes (the smaller, egg shaped ones)
- 2 small cans hearts of palm, drained
- 5 eggs
- ¼ cup flat leaf parsley, chopped
- ½ cup sliced black olives
- ½ cup onion, minced
- ⅔ cup cream, warmed
- 1 tablespoon Dijon mustard
- 2 teaspoons Italian seasoning
- 1 cup mozzarella cheese, shredded
- Salt/Freshly grated black pepper

Preheat oven to 375 F.

Cut the hearts of palm to the same height as the tomatoes. Slice the tops off the tomatoes and carefully scoop out the flesh. Insert the hearts of palm into the tomatoes and slice a little off the bottom end of the tomatoes so that they can sit up without tipping over. Sit the tomatoes upright over the bottom of the pie shell.

In a bowl, whisk the remaining ingredients and pour slowly around the tomatoes in the pie shell. Bake 35-40 minutes.

Makes 6-8 servings.

OLIVE OIL QUICHE DOUGH:

If you're in a bind for time, this will do the trick.
- 2 cups whole wheat flour
- ½ teaspoon salt
- 2/3 cup olive oil
- 2/3 cup milk, warmed

Mix the flour and salt in a food processor. Slowly pour in the olive oil and milk, mixing until a dough is formed. Transfer dough to a floured surface and knead in a little more flour if the dough is not stiff enough.

Separate the dough into two balls and roll to fit a 10 inch pie plate.
Makes 2 pie shells

Soups

At the Café we have become known for our soups. People know that when the meal starts off this well, it is a good indication of things to come. Soups are easy to decorate with a cheese straw, a squeeze of cream from a plastic bottle wiggled into a pattern with a fork, snipped fresh herbs or anything 'edibly' imaginable. I have included some of our favorite garnishes.

CREAM OF CARROT SOUP:

Simplicity perfected.
    2 tablespoons butter
    3 cups carrots, diced
    ½ cup onion, chopped
    6 cups chicken broth
    2 tablespoons rice
    ½ cup heavy cream
    Salt/Freshly ground black pepper
    cream and chopped parsley for garnish

    In large saucepan, sauté the carrots and onion in butter until soft, 5 minutes. Add the broth, rice, salt and pepper. Bring to a boil, reduce heat and simmer for 30 minutes.

Purée in the blender then return to saucepan and add the heavy cream. Heat without boiling. Ladle into serving bowls and give a squirt of cream over the surface (make a pattern with a knife if desired) then sprinkle a little parsley.

Serve with a cheese twist.
>Makes 6-8 servings

Note: Add 1 tablespoon minced, fresh ginger to the carrots and onions to make this soup into a "Cream of Carrot and Ginger."

LENTIL AND TOMATO SOUP:

A hearty, spicy soup. Make enough for seconds.
- 2 cloves garlic, minced
- 4 bacon strips, cut up
- 1 onion, diced
- 1 celery stalk, diced
- 28 oz tomatoes, diced, drained
- 8 oz package lentils
- 6 cups chicken broth
- 1 bay leaf
- 1 teaspoon crushed red pepper
- ¼ cup parsley, chopped
- Salt/Freshly ground black pepper

In large saucepan, sauté the bacon over medium until the fat is rendered. Remove bacon to paper towel. In bacon fat, sauté the onions, celery and garlic for 3 minutes. Add the tomatoes, lentils, broth, bay leaf and spices. Bring to a boil, then simmer 1 hour 15 minutes. Add the parsley and bacon. Serve with cheddar toasts.

    Makes 6-8 servings

BANGKOK SOUP:

This exotic soup is our most popular and it is surprisingly easy to make if you use canned soup as a base instead of preparing your own .
- 2 x 19 oz chicken and rice soup (ready to serve)
- 1 teaspoon Thai red chili sauce
- 1 teaspoon lemon pepper seasoning
- 2 cups bokchoy or chinese lettuce, finely chopped
- 14 oz can coconut milk
- 1 lemon, sliced ½ inch thick

In large saucepan, combine the soups, chili sauce, seasoning and lettuce. Bring to a boil and simmer 10 minutes. Add the coconut milk and simmer 5 minutes more.

Quarter the lemon slices. Ladle the soup into bowls and top with the lemon quarters.
        Makes 4-6 servings

Note: For Seafood Bangkok, you can toss in 1½ cups frozen shrimp at the same time as the coconut milk.

ESCARGOT AND MUSHROOM SOUP:

If you like escargot in garlic butter, you'll love this soup.
- 11 tablespoons butter
- ½ cup onion, finely chopped
- 4 cups mushrooms, sliced
- 5 cups chicken broth
- 2 potatoes, peeled, cubed
- ¼ cup flour
- 2 cups cream, 35% or 15%
- 6 oz can escargots, chopped
- ¼ cup parsley, chopped
- 2 green onions, minced
- 2 cloves garlic, minced
- ½ cup dry white wine
- Salt/Freshly ground black pepper

In frying pan, sauté onions and mushrooms in 2 tablespoons butter until soft, 5 minutes.

In large saucepan, put the chicken broth, potatoes and sautéed mushrooms and onions. Bring to a boil and simmer for 20 minutes.

In medium saucepan, melt 6 tablespoons butter over medium heat. Stir in the flour until well blended. Add the cream and stir until thick. Season with salt and pepper. Add to the mushroom mixture.

In the original frying pan, sauté the escargots, parsley, green onions and garlic in the butter until tender. Add to the mushroom-cream mixture.

Add the white wine and heat through without boiling. Season with salt and pepper.

Makes 8 servings

ARIZONA CORN AND RED PEPPER SOUP:

The color and the texture of this soup is unique and unexpected. The best two words to describe the taste is "Oh, man!"

2 tablespoons butter
1 red pepper, chopped fine
1 onion, chopped fine
3 garlic cloves, minced
14½ oz can diced tomatoes (do not drain)
2 cups chicken broth
2 tablespoons chipotle chillies, canned
2 x 14.5 oz cans creamed corn
16 oz frozen corn
1 cup heavy cream
1 teaspoon oregano
Salt/Freshly ground black pepper
Marbled cheddar cheese, grated, for garnish

In large saucepan, over medium heat, sauté the red pepper, onions and garlic in butter until soft, 5 minutes. Add the tomatoes, sauté 2 minutes more.

In a blender, purée the broth and chillies. Add to saucepan with the creamed corn. Bring to a boil, reduce heat to medium and simmer for 15 minutes. Add frozen corn, cream, oregano, salt and pepper. Simmer 5 minutes.

Ladle into bowls and garnish with grated cheese.
        Makes 6 servings

CREAM OF HEART OF PALM SOUP:

Meditteranean style comfort food.
    1 tablespoon butter
    14 oz can heart of palm, chopped
    1 onion, diced
    1 garlic clove, minced
    1 potato, peeled, diced
    1 teaspoon flour
    3 cups chicken broth
    1 cup heavy cream
    1 egg yolk
    Salt/Freshly ground black pepper
    Butter shaving, for garnish

In large saucepan, sauté the hearts of palm, onion, garlic and potato in the butter until soft, a few minutes. Salt and pepper to taste. Incorporate the flour and cook, stirring for a minute or two. Pour in the chicken broth and bring to a boil. Reduce heat and simmer 15 minutes.

In the meantime, vigorously whisk the cream and egg yolk together. Add salt and pepper if desired. Slowly add to the broth, stirring constantly.

Simmer 5 minutes (you can pass it in a blender, if desired). Ladle into bowls and garnish with a butter shaving and freshly ground black pepper.
    Makes 4 servings

Serve with eggplant crisps

ONION SOUP "AU GRATIN":

French style comfort food.
- ¼ cup butter
- 8 red onions, sliced
- 2 cloves garlic, minced
- 12 oz bottle beer, pale
- 3 cups beef broth
- ½ teaspoon sage, dried
- 1 tablespoon tomato paste
- 4-6 slices French baguette, toasted
- 1½ cups aged cheddar, grated
- Parsley, chopped for garnish
- Salt/Freshly ground black pepper

Sauté the onions in the butter over medium-low heat until caramelized, about 12-15 minutes. Add the garlic and cook 1 minute more. Add the beer, broth, sage and tomato paste. Bring to a boil, reduce heat and simmer for 15 minutes. Season with salt and pepper.

Ladle the soup into 4 ovenproof bowls. Cover with the sliced, toasted bread, top with the cheese then sprinkle with the parsley. Pass under the broiler until the cheese is melted and browned.

Makes 4 servings

Note: You can wear motorcycle goggles when slicing a large quantity of onions to save your eyes. I do. I'm not joking!

Soup Garnishes

Cheddar Toast:

Lay a piece of toast directly on the surface of the soup.

> 1 French baguette, sliced on a long diagonal, 1 inch thick
> Butter
> 6 tablespoons Dijon mustard
> 1 cup aged Cheddar cheese, grated

Preheat broiler.

Arrange the baguette slices on a baking sheet. Spread with butter. Broil until golden, about 1 minute. Spread the buttered side with Dijon mustard, then cover with cheddar.

Place under the broiler again until the cheese is melted and bubbly.
Makes 6 servings

Lace Cheese Crisps:
Dainty and delicious

> 2 cups Parmigianno Reggiano, grated
> 1 teaspoon fennel seeds

Preheat oven to 375° F.

In bowl, mix the cheese and the seeds.

On parchment lined baking sheets, spread the cheese to form 4 inch rounds. Bake 6-8 minutes. When cool enough to handle, lay them over a rolling pin to give them a curved shape.

Makes 12 crisps

EGGPLANT CHIPS:

Watch out! These are as addictive as potato chips.
   3 tablespoons icing sugar
   3 tablespoons cornstarch
   ½ cup panko or dry breadcrumbs
   pinch salt
   1 medium eggplant (thin variety), sliced into rounds paper-thin, with a slicer
   Vegetable oil for frying

In bowl, whisk together icing sugar, cornstarch, breadcrumbs and salt. Fill a deep, heavy skillet with oil to a depth of three inches. Heat over medium and try to maintain the temperature around 360° F.

Dredge eggplant on both sides in cornstarch mixture and fry in batches for 2 minutes, turning occasionally for even cooking. Drain on paper towels and sprinkle with kosher salt.
   Makes 6 servings

HERBED BARLEY:

This adds color and crunch to dress up any cream soup.
    2 tablespoons olive oil
    2 cloves garlic
    ½ cup pearl barley
    1 teaspoon fresh tarragon, minced
    2 teaspoon fresh chives, minced
    2 teaspoon parsley, minced
    Salt/Freshly ground black pepper

Sauté the garlic cloves in the olive oil over medium heat until the oil is aromatic. Remove the garlic and discard. Add the barley, tarragon, chives and parsley to the oil and sauté 2 minutes. Season with salt and pepper.
    Makes 4 servings

CHEESE STRAWS:

I always lay a cheese straw diagonally across the corner of the soup bowl. It's an easy way to add a dramatic effect.

- 2 sheets frozen puff pastry, defrosted in fridge overnight
- 1 egg
- 1 tablespoon water
- ½ cup parmesan, grated
- 1 cup Swiss cheese, grated
- 1 teaspoon fresh thyme, minced
- Salt/Freshly ground black pepper

Preheat over to 375° F.

Make an egg wash by whisking the egg and water together. On a lightly floured board, roll each sheet into a 10 x 12 inch rectangle. Brush each pastry sheet with the egg wash then sprinkle, diving evenly, with parmesan, Swiss, thyme, salt and pepper. Cut each sheet crossways into 12 strips. With fingers, twist, the strips and lay them on a parchment lined baking sheet.

Bake 10-15 minutes, turn straws over and bake 2 minutes more.
Makes 24 strips

SALADS

At the Café, the only salad we originally offered as a meal was the "Chicken Thai Salad." All the others were sides. That quickly had to change. We now offer an assorted plate of salads because it was too difficult for the customers to choose only one. The customer is always right!

ORANGE FENNEL SALAD:

Tastes like orange licorice–if orange licorice existed.
    2 bulbs fennel, sliced ½ inch thick
    ½ red onion, thinly sliced
    * 3 oranges, segmented
    ¼ cup olive oil
    2 tablespoons Dijon mustard
    ¼ cup flat leaf parsley, chopped
    1 tablespoon lemon juice
    Salt/Freshly ground black pepper

    In large bowl, put fennel, onions and oranges. In small bowl, whisk olive oil, Dijon, parsley, lemon juice, salt and pepper. Pour over fennel-orange mixture and toss lightly to mix.

    Pour onto serving platter.
            Makes 6 large servings

* **Technique for Segmenting Oranges:**

(1) Slice the top and bottom off fruit
(2) Stand orange up on one flat end and slice down, following curve of the fruit, removing peel and white pith.
(3) Lay orange on its side and slice into 5 mm. rounds then cut the rounds in half creating half moon shapes.

CHICKEN THAI SALAD:

This is our hot number and I believe the secret is in the sauce.

Salad:

    2 cups spring salad or mesclun
    * 1 large orange, segmented
    ½ red pepper, julienned
    1 green onion, thinly sliced on the diagonal
    2 chicken breasts, cooked, sliced on the diagonal
    ½ cup bean sprouts
    2 tbsp roasted peanuts, shelled

Using two salad plates, layer each plate with 1 cup salad, half the red peppers, half the green onions. Lay one chicken breast in the center of the plate. Position four orange segments in each corner of the plate. Sprinkle with half the bean sprouts and scatter half the peanuts over the surface. Serve with the peanut sauce.

        Makes 2 large servings

Peanut Sauce:

    ½ cup peanut butter
    ½ cup boiling water
    2 tablespoon soya sauce
    ½ teaspoon dry mustard powder
    2 tablespoons lime juice
    1 teaspoon crushed red chili flakes
    1 garlic clove, minced
    2 tablespoons sesame oil

Whisk all.

* The technique for segmenting oranges is given in the recipe for "Orange Fennel Salad."

BOWTIE PASTA SALAD WITH PESTO, OLIVES AND SUN DRIED TOMATOES:

Spectacular and simple–the title is almost as long as the recipe.

4 cups Bowtie pasta, cooked
* ½ cup pesto
½ cup sun dried tomatoes, drained, halved
½ cup Kalmata olives, pitted
¼ cup Parmigiana–Regganio, shaved

Combine the pasta, pesto, tomatoes, olives and toss well. Divide among serving plates and garnish with the cheese shavings.
Makes 4 large servings

* Pesto:

4 cups fresh basil leaves
½ cup olive oil
⅓ cup pine nuts
2 garlic cloves
½ cup parmesan cheese, grated
1 teaspoon kosher salt

In blender, combine basil, olive oil, pine nuts and garlic and blend, stopping often to push leaves down until paste forms. Add cheese and salt; blend until smooth.
Makes 1 cup

Note: I prefer to use a blender rather than a food processor as the pesto has a smoother texture when blended.

GREEK SALAD:

Because of the red wine vinegar add the feta cheese last, unless you want pink cheese.

    2 pints cherry tomatoes, halved
    1 English cucumber
    ½ red onion, diced
    ½ cup Kalmata olives, pitted
    ¼ cup red wine vinegar
    ¼ cup olive oil
    1 teaspoon oregano
    Salt/Freshly ground black pepper
    1 cup feta cheese, cubed

In a large bowl, combine tomatoes, cucumber, red onions and olives.

In separate bowl, whisk the vinegar, oil, oregano, salt and pepper. Add to the tomato mixture and toss lightly to combine. Add the feta.
        Makes 6 large servings

Note: Olive oil congeals in the fridge so if you're not using all of it right away, replace the olive oil with canola oil.

144　　Have a Java

COOL CUCUMBER MINT SALAD:

Even the color is refreshing–cool mint green.
    3 English cucumbers, halved, seeded, sliced thick
    1 teaspoon lemon juice
    2 avocadoes, peeled, pitted, sliced
    3 green onions, sliced
    1 tablespoon crushed mint
    ¼ cup mayonnaise
    kosher salt

In large bowl, put the cucumbers, green onions and avocadoes then toss with the lemon juice. Gently stir in the mayonnaise and mint. Season with salt.
        Makes 6 large servings

SPINACH COUSCOUS SALAD:

This delicious salad is best served at room temperature.
- 5 cups couscous, cooked, cooled
- 2 cups spinach, thinly sliced
- ¾ cup golden raisins
- ¾ cup almonds, toasted

Vinaigrette:

- 3 tablespoons balsamic vinegar
- 3 tablespoons orange juice
- ⅓ cup olive oil
- 1 tablespoon ground cumin
- Salt/Freshly ground black pepper

In large mixing bowl, combine couscous, spinach, raisins and almonds.

In separate bowl, whisk the vinaigrette ingredients. Pour dressing over couscous and toss to mix.

Makes 6 sidedish servings

ROASTED CURRIED HARVEST VEGETABLE SALAD:

Fills your home with a mouth watering aroma.
    2 cups baby carrots, whole or halved
    12 cups cauliflowerrettes
    1 large red onion, cut into wedges
    2 potatoes, scrubbed, cut into wedges
    1 teaspoon ground coriander
    1 teaspoon ground cumin
    ¾ cup olive oil
    ½ cup red wine vinegar
    3½ teaspoons curry powder
    1 tablespoon hot paprika
    1¾ teaspoons salt
    parsley, for garnish
Preheat oven to 450° F.

In large mixing bowl put carrots, cauliflower, red onion and potatoes.

In separate bowl, whisk together all remaining ingredients. Pour over vegetables and toss to mix. Transfer vegetables to baking sheets, in a single layer, pouring all dressing over vegetables. Roast; turning occasionally for about 30-40 minutes.

Mound on serving platter and garnish with parsley.
        Makes 8-10 sidedish servings

148   Have a Java

Sandwiches

European style coffee shops don't offer many ordinary sandwiches. The paninis and baguettes are filled with the best quality meats, cheeses and the freshest vegetables. It's a winning formula. For home, I would definitely recommend investing in a panini press because you'll be "hard pressed" to make a great panini sandwich without one.

CARAMELIZED ONION BAGUETTE:

This sounds too simple to be as good as it is.
- 1 french baguette, split in half
- 4 tablespoons butter
- 2 red onions, sliced
- 12 anchovies, chopped
- 1 teaspoon brown sugar
- 2 tablespoon fresh thyme, chopped
- 2 tablespoons olive oil
- 1/3 cup Kalmata olives, pitted
- 1/3 cup Parmigiano-Reggiano

Preheat oven to 450° F.

In skillet, over medium heat, sauté onions, anchovies, brown sugar, thyme, salt and pepper in butter until caramelized, about 20 minutes.

Cut ends off the baguette and place, cut sides up, on a baking sheet and brush both sides with the olive oil. Spread the onion mixture on both sides and distribute the olives evenly over the surface.

Bake in oven for 12 minutes and sprinkle the cheese shavings over the top.
Makes 2 servings

ROAST BEEF AND BLUE CHEESE ROLLS:

A great sandwich for beef lovers everywhere.
- 4 Italian rolls, split in half
- 12 slices roast beef
- Salt/Fresh ground black pepper
- Arugula leaves

Blue Cheese Mayonnaise:

- $^2/_3$ cup sour cream
- ¼ cup creamy blue cheese
- $^1/_3$ cup mayonnaise
- ½ teaspoon worcesteshire sauce
- Salt/Freshly ground black pepper

Combine all mayonnaise ingredients and blend well. Spread both halves of rolls with the mayonnaise, layer the slices of roast beef, arugula leaves, salt and pepper.
  Makes 4 servings

Note: For those who don't like blue cheese, make a "**Horseradish Sauce**" by combining: 1 cup sour cream
  1 Tablespoon horseradish
  Olive oil, a drizzle
  salt/pepper, to taste

152   Have a Java

PRESSED VEGETABLE ROLLS:

Why does pressing the sandwich accentuate the flavor so much? I have no idea–it just does.

    4 french rolls, about 6 inches long
    4 tablespoons pesto
    4 tablespoons olive oil
    4 tablespoons red wine vinegar
    1 cup roasted red peppers, drained
    12 oz mozzarella, sliced
    2 tomatoes, sliced
    16 Kalmata olives, pitted
    Arugula leaves
    Salt/Freshly ground black pepper

Prepare each sandwich as follows:

Split rolls in half but not all the way through. Spread 1 tablespoon pesto on bottom half and pour 1 tablespoon olive oil and 1 tablespoon red wine vinegar on top half.

On pesto half, layer ¼ cup roasted red peppers, 3 oz sliced mozzarella and ½ tomato, sliced. Season with salt and pepper. Top tomatoes with four olives and arugula leaves. Close the sandwiches and roll tightly in plastic wrap. Lay sandwiches on a baking sheet and cover with another baking sheet. Place heavy cans to completely cover the top baking sheet. Let sandwiches compress for 6 hours at room temperature.
        Makes 4 servings

ARANCINI:

Not technically a sandwich, more like a meat and cheese stuffed rice ball, but its an Italian Coffee Shop classic.

    2 cups water
    1 teaspoon saffron threads
    1½ cups Arborio rice
    ½ cup parmesan, grated
    2 tablespoons butter
    3 eggs
    8 oz mozzarella, cut into 6 cubes
    ½ cup pepperoni or salami, diced
    ¼ cup flour
    1 cup dry seasoned breadcrumbs
    vegetable oil for frying

Bring the water and saffron to a boil. Add the rice, reduce heat to low and simmer 20 minutes, stirring often, until water is absorbed. Stir in the parmesan and butter and let cool completely. Beat 1 egg and stir in rice mixture. Form rice into six balls, inserting the mozzarella and meat in the center and reforming into balls.

Pour vegetable oil in a heavy saucepan to measure 3 inches deep. Heat to 375° F.

Take three separate bowls. Put the flour in the first bowl, the remaining two eggs, beaten, in the second and the dry breadcrumbs in the third. Roll the rice balls in the flour, then in the eggs and then the breadcrumbs. Fry in batches, in the oil, for 5 minutes each.

Serve as is or top with tomato sauce and some more parmesan.
        Makes 6 servings

BRUSCHETTA AND BRIE BAGUETTE:

This turns lunch into an elegant luncheon.
>   1 french baguette, split in two
>   *1 cup bruschetta
>   12 oz brie, sliced

Preheat broiler.

Cut ends off baguette and place on a baking sheet, cut sides up. Spread bruschetta over bread and top with sliced brie. Pass under a broiler until cheese is slightly melted but still recognizable as brie.
>   Makes 2 servings

Bruschetta

>   ½ red onion, finely chopped
>   3 plum tomatoes, halved, seeded, finely chopped
>   2 garlic cloves, minced
>   20 fresh basil leaves, chopped
>   4 tablespoons olive oil
>   Salt/Freshly ground black pepper

Combine all ingredients and mix well.

ITALIAN PANINI:

Serve the sandwich with sliced tomatoes and lettuce on the side so they can be added after heating in the panini press.

    2 ciabatta (panini) breads, split in half
    2 teaspoons prepared mustard
    4 slices capicollo
    4 slices mortadello
    2 slices prosciutto
    2 slices provolone cheese

Preheat panini press.

    Spread mustard on bottom halves of ciabattas. Layer with two slices capicollo, two slices mortadello, one slice prosciutto and one slice provolone. Close the sandwiches and grill in a panini press until golden and heated through.

        Makes 2 servings

EGGPLANT, HUMMUS AND FETA CIABATTA:

A thin, spicy, vegetarian sandwich.
- 4 ciabatta (panini) breads, split in half
- 1 cup marinated, spicy eggplant, drained
- *¼ cup hummus
- 12 oz crumbled Feta
- 4 tablespoons olive oil
- 2 tablespoons fresh mint, chopped
- Salt/Freshly ground black pepper

Preheat panini press.

Spread hummus over bottom halves of breads. Top with the eggplant, feta, salt, pepper and mint. Drizzle the olive oil over the top halves of the breads. Close the sandwiches and grill in a panini press until bread is golden and heated through.

Makes 4 servings

* **Hummus:**

- 1 teaspoon ground cumin
- 4 garlic cloves, crushed
- 2 cups canned chickpeas, drained
- 1½ teaspoons salt
- ⅓ cup tahini paste
- 6 tablespoons fresh lemon juice
- 2 tablespoons water
- 1 teaspoon hot pepper sauce, or to taste

Place chickpeas, garlic, cumin, tahini paste, salt and lemon juice in a food processor and process until combined. Add water and hot pepper sauce and process until smooth. If serving as an hors d'oeuvre, put on a serving platter, drizzle with olive oil sprinkle with paprika.

SMOKED SALMON PUMPERNICKEL CLUB:

A special occasion club sandwich.
    4 large slices pumpernickel, toasted
    8-12 slices smoked salmon
    4 tablespoons cream cheese, soft
    2 tablespoons capers, drained
    1 tomato, thinly sliced
    Boston lettuce leaves
    Salt/Freshly ground black pepper

Spread 2 slices of toasted pumpernickel with half the cream cheese. Cut the slices in half to obtain 4 pieces of toast. Set one of the pieces aside. Cover the remaining three pieces with half the smoked salmon, half the capers, half the tomato, leaves of lettuce then sprinkle with salt and pepper. Stack the salmon-tomato toasts one on top of the other. Top with the reserved toast, cream cheese side down. Secure with a toothpick.

Repeat process for the other sandwich.
    Makes 2 servings

Sandwiches 159

Index

Arancini   154

Bagel, ricotta   110

Baguette:

    Bacon and egg   111

    Bruschetta and brie   155

    Onion, caramelized   149

Barley, herbed   137

Bars:

    Blondies   61

    Butter   65

    Oatcakes   66

Biscotti:

    Almond   22

    Chocolate pistachio   24

    Chocolate, triple   21

    Orange chocolate   23

    Orange cranberry   19

Bread, Sweet Loaf:

    Banana   42

    Carrot   44

    Lemon nut   43

Brownie:

    Gooey fudgey peanut butter   59

    Chocolate, triple   68

Bruschetta   155

Butter:

    Maple Syrup   31

    Moka   111

Cappuccino:

    Iced cappuccino   10

    Mochaccino   10

    Soyaccino   10

Cake:

    Carrot, Mango Tango   105

    Chocolate Amaretto   104

    Chocolate banana   70

    Chocolate, caramel Skyscraper   106

    Chocolate Coca Cola   77

    Cheesecake, creamy   109

    Cinnamon streusel coffee   101

    Coconut, Coco Bango   108

    Lemon Blueberry   74

Orange walnut streusel	72
Praline	75
Tiramisu	99
Whiskey Tipsy fudge	102

Cheese:

Straws	138
Lace crisps	134

Cheesecake cup, no bake — 92

Chips, eggplant — 136

Ciabatta, eggplant, hummus and feta — 157

Cinnamon Buns — 48

Coffee Cocktails:

Affogato	17
Café Napoleon	17
Café Yukatan	17
Creamy Dreamy Martini	16
Coffee Cream Whiskey	17
Con Leche Shake	17
Espresso Martini	16
Latte Royale	17
Martini-cinno	16

Cookie:

Chocolate chip, classic	54
Chocolate ginger	53
Oatmeal raisin	56

Peanut butter oatmeal	50
Sugar	57
White chocolate coconut macadamia	52

Crème Brulee — 90

Crepes:

Apricot brandy	114
Nutella banana	113

Crisp — 80

Croissant, ham and brie — 112

Dough:

Hot and spicy quiche	122
Olive oil quiche	125

Espresso:

Americano	7
Breve	8
Con Panna	8
Corretto	8
Dopio	7
Lungo	7
Macchiato	7
Red Eye	8
Ristretto	7
Romano	8
Spicy Viennese	8

Financier — 46

Frappe — 10

Frosting:
- Caramel — 106
- Chocolate — 106
- Chocolate buttercream — 69
- White chocolate buttercream — 69

Ham, Morning Glory eggs and — 115

Hot Chocolate:
- Bittersweet — 14
- White — 14

Hummus — 157

Latte:
- Café Mocha — 12
- Caramel Viennese — 12
- Chai — 12
- Eggnog — 13
- Five Layer — 13
- Flavored — 12
- Gingerbread — 13
- Mango — 13
- Mocha — 13
- Three Layer — 12
- Viennese — 12

Macaroon, chocolate — 58

Milk:

    Frothing   5

    Textured   4

    Texturing   4

    Texturing without a machine   5

    Steaming   4

Mojito Granita   93

Moka Butter   111

Muffin:

    Blueberry   40

    Carrot, tropical   37

    Chocolate, triple   36

    Cranberry orange   38

    Lemon poppyseed   33

    Oatmeal date   39

    Rhubarb   35

Panini, Italian   156

Parfait, fruit and yogurt   94

Pastry Dough, perfect   86

Pesto   142

Pie:

    Apple, Mile High   80

    Coconut cream   83

    Keylime, double   79

    Pecan bourbon   78

Pound Cake, Irish Cream ... 47

Pudding:

    Bread with bourbon sauce ... 89

    Rice ... 87

    Rum raisin, rice ... 88

Pumpernickel Club, smoked salmon ... 158

Quiche:

    Bacon and leek ... 117

    Crab, killer ... 119

    Italian Tomato and Heart of Palm ... 124

    Spinach mushroom and bacon ... 120

    Tex-Mex ... 123

    Three Cheese Asparagus ... 121

Rolls:

    Roast beef, blue cheese ... 151

    Vegetable, pressed ... 153

Salad:

    Bowtie pasta with pesto, olives and sun dried tomatoes ... 142

    Chicken Thai ... 141

    Couscous spinach ... 146

    Cucumber mint, cool ... 145

    Greek ... 143

    Orange fennel ... 139

    Vegetable, roasted, curried, Harvest ... 147

Scone:

Apple date	28
Blueberry	26
Oatmeal	30
Orange chocolate chip	29
Raisin	31

Soup:

Arizona Corn and Red Pepper	131
Bangkok	129
Cream of Carrot	126
Cream of Heart of Palm	132
Escargot and Mushroom	130
Lentil and Tomato	128
Onion Soup "au gratin"	133

Square:

Chocolate peanut butter	63
Date	64

Streusel   72

Tart:

Fruit and Cream	82
Raisin butter	84
Rhubarb almond	81

Toast, cheddar   134

Vanilla Sugar   46

978-0-595-43296-7
0-595-43296-4